The Mallon Crew

Vic Jay

The Mallon Crew

DEDICATION

This book is dedicated to all the men and women of Bomber Command,
particularly those of No. 75 (New Zealand) Squadron.

The Mallon Crew

CONTENTS

The Mallon Crew

ACKNOWLEDGMENTS

This book could not have been written without the support and generosity of the following people: Barrie and Kevin Mallon, Ruth Ryan and her sisters Maryann and Penny, Yvonne and Warren Wairau, Wendy Edson and Allan and David Philp have all been generous with their time and with their families' memories. Particularly valuable have been the letters written by Ruth's father, Jim Haworth, and the interview Bill Mallon gave at the age of eighty four to Martin Halliday of the New Zealand Defence Force 'Military Oral History Project'. I thank the Air Force Museum of New Zealand for providing me with the transcript.

Pete Tresadern, who painstakingly researched the story of his partner's grandfather, Cecil Butler, a Lancaster flight engineer shot down and killed on his 31st operation, provided me with masses of invaluable information about flight engineer training and kindly let me use whatever I needed.

Simon Sommerville, who created a blog about No. 75(NZ) Squadron that is a lasting memorial to his late father Bob, not only inspired me to pursue this project but also helped countless other families learn more about the contributions made by their loved ones in the squadron. Chris Newey, whose uncle Gerry flew with the squadron in 1944-45, Glen Turner of the 75 Squadron Association (N.Z.) and Peter Wheeler of the New Zealand Bomber Command Association have frequently steered me in the right direction, selflessly assisted by Dave Homewood and contributors to the 'Wings over New Zealand' forum.

I should also like to express my thanks to Doug and Janet Williamson, who allowed me to include Doug's remarkable story in this book, and to Stephanie Gibbons, the library manager at New Plymouth Boys' High School, for whom nothing was too much trouble. Thanks also to all those other individuals who made a contribution, however small, to this project – and there were many of them.

Finally, I have to thank my brother, Bob, and sister, Pam, for filling in some of the gaps in our dad's story and my wife, Sally, for her patience during the hundreds of hours I've spent at my laptop over the last four years.

AUTHOR'S NOTE

'The Mallon Crew' is the extraordinary result of four years' research. My decision in 2012 to write a blog about my dad's war-time experiences as the flight engineer of a Lancaster bomber took me on an incredible voyage of discovery and unearthed some remarkable stories of courage, sacrifice and betrayal.

As a child growing up in the 1950s, I never tired of asking my dad what he did in the war. I wanted to know all about his role, what flak was like and even how aircraft were able to fly. By the time I left primary school, my interest had started to wane and, when he died in 1974 at the age of just fifty five, I thought I had lost any chance of discovering more about this period of his life. I couldn't have been more mistaken.

Nearly forty years later, with just a handful of photographs, his log book and the name of his New Zealand pilot, Bill Mallon, my modest research project into 'Bob Jay's war' uncovered more tragedies than I could have imagined possible and connected me with the families of all but one of my dad's crew. It even gave me the opportunity to talk to a man of ninety four who had flown with my dad and to discover a photograph of his crew's aircraft flying to its last target.

This book is not about a squadron, nor is it about individual acts of heroism, it is about a small group of unremarkable men thrown together briefly during the last few months of the war and the amazing way in which their stories have unfolded seventy years later. They survived the war but their lives would never be the same again. I defy anyone not to be moved by their experiences or to marvel at the power of the internet to bring people together.

CREW LISTS

THE MALLON CREW

Pilot: Flight Sergeant **William Mallon** (R.N.Z.A.F. 427521), aged 24 (1920 – 2010)

Navigator: Flight Sergeant **James Randel Haworth** (R.N.Z.A.F. 4216510), aged 34 (1911 – 2001)

Bomb aimer: Flying Officer **Kenneth Ralph Philp** (R.N.Z.A.F. 429093), aged 31 (1913 -1991)

Wireless operator: Flight Sergeant **Frank (Tinker) Symes** (R.N.Z.A.F. 428164), aged 20 (1924 – 1979)

Flight engineer: Sergeant **Robert Alfred Jay** (R.A.F.V.R. 1596172), aged 25 (1919 – 1974)

Mid-upper gunner: Sergeant **Don Cook** (R.A.F.V.R.), aged 20 (? - ?)

Rear gunner: Sergeant **Denis William Eynstone** (R.A.F.V.R. 1606772), aged 19 (1925 – 2011)

Mid-under gunner (first three operations only)**:** Flying Officer **Charles Frederick Green D.F.C.** (R.A.F.V.R. 178730) aged 23 (born in 1921 and the only one known to be still alive at the time of writing)

Pilot after Bill's departure: Flight Lieutenant **Eric Frank Butler** (R.N.Z.A.F. 425558), aged 27 (1917 – 1994)

Bomb aimer (after Ken's transfer): Flying Officer **Lancelot Osgood Waugh** (R.N.ZA.F. 429021), aged 30 (1914 – 1994)

Bomb aimer (for one operation): Flying Officer **Owen Charles Willetts** (R.N.Z.A.F. 425964), aged 23 (1922 – 1994)

THE TAYLOR CREW

On April 4th 1945 Bob flew as flight engineer with the following crew, made up of British, Australian and Canadian airmen:

Pilot: Flight Lieutenant **Ian Taylor** (R.A.F.V.R. 1550767/135709)

Navigator: Pilot Officer **David Dickson Hope** (R.A.A.F. 401954)

Bomb aimer: Warrant Officer **John Alfred Tarran** (R.A.A.F. 419395)

Wireless operator: Warrant Officer **Mervyn John King** (R.A.A.F. 430036)

Mid-upper gunner: Flight Sergeant **William (Bill) Henry Grout** (R.C.A.F. R109214)

Rear gunner: Sergeant **E. Franklin** (R.A.F.V.R.)

Their usual flight engineer, **Sergeant L. Deeprose** (R.A.F.V.R.), was unavailable for this operation.

1 AN INCREDIBLE JOURNEY

Bob Jay (20) striding along Cleethorpes promenade, summer 1939

In **April 2012**, thirty eight years after my dad's death, I experienced the thrill of a taxi run on board Lancaster NX611 at East Kirkby in my home county of Lincolnshire. A spark was lit and my curiosity about my dad's war service was re-ignited. I decided I needed answers to questions I had never asked about his brief relationship with this iconic aircraft. He had died in 1974 and the only clues he had left to help in my search were a handful of photographs, his log book and the name of his New Zealand pilot, Bill Mallon.

I decided to research and record as much as I could of his war-time experiences, not just for my sake but also for his grandchildren and great grandchildren, none of whom knew him and for whom the Second World War was ancient history. This decision took me on an incredible voyage of discovery which extended way beyond my dad's story. What was intended to be a single entry blog, 'Bob Jay's war', for the benefit of close family grew to more than forty chapters containing over 50,000 words and so far has been visited over 20,000 times.

Shortly after returning home from East Kirkby, I ordered a copy of my dad's death certificate and applied to the R.A.F. for his service record. While I was waiting, I discovered the 'Lancaster Archive' forum, unfortunately no longer active, on which I found a picture of my dad's squadron, No. 75(NZ) Squadron, taken in March 1945 and posted by Simon Sommerville. Simon had recently lost his father, also called Bob, a bomb aimer with the squadron who had completed a tour of thirty operations in 1943 before re-joining the squadron for a second tour in 1944. As a way of dealing with his father's death Simon had started to research his war service and the results of this project can be seen in his impressive blog '75nzsquadron.wordpress.com'.

Simon, currently the course leader for the MA (Hons) Product Design course at the University of Central Lancashire, sent me a high resolution copy of the squadron photograph and, to my disappointment, my dad was nowhere to be seen. I later discovered that it was taken during the period when the Mallon crew were away for a week's training in the latest navigation technology, followed by six days leave. However, Simon was able to provide valuable information about the squadron and he sent me what was probably the most valuable of all the resources I had during those early days, the squadron's Operations Record Book (O.R.B.) for 1945.

The O.R.B. contains information on every aspect of the squadron's work and, with the help of my dad's log book, I was able to discover the details of every one of the crew's operations, including the bombs they carried, their targets, the aircraft they flew, the times of take-off and landing and any other significant events. Most important of all though, I discovered the names of the rest of the crew.

The O.R.B. entry for the 24th April 1945 showing details of the operation and the names of the Mallon crew

As my dad was a flight engineer, Simon then suggested I take a look at another blog, 'Aircraft Q failed to return' (*rafww2butler.wordpress.com*), compiled by Pete Tresadern. Pete had responded to a throwaway comment by his partner's mum that she would love to know more about her father, Cecil Butler, who had died when she was a baby. The family had no diaries or log book to help in the search but Pete's training as a business analyst kicked in and the end result is a wonderful tribute to Cecil, who was killed on his thirty first operation with No. 35 'Pathfinder' Squadron in February 1945.

I contacted Pete in **May 2012** and discovered that he had researched Cecil's route from civilian to fully qualified flight engineer so thoroughly that a large part of my work had already been done and he generously allowed me to use this material in my blog.

The following month, I took advantage of a trip to Cambridgeshire to visit the museum on the 'Lancaster Business Park' at Witchford to view its collection of memorabilia from the R.A.F. stations at Mepal and Witchford. One of the pictures on display was one I had at home and it had been puzzling me for months. It was of just thirty seven airmen, too few to be a squadron or a flight, standing in front of a Lancaster. It included my dad and the caption alongside it, '*75 Squadron Pilots and Flight Engineers May 1945*', solved the riddle.

An interesting postscript to this discovery took nearly two years for me to spot. Shortly after my trip to Witchford Simon posted details of an e-mail he had received from Paul Reay, the grandson of Les Hofert, also a flight engineer with the squadron in 1945, together with a close-up of Les taken from the squadron photograph of March 1945. It was 2014 before I realised that in the picture I had seen at Witchford Les is standing next to my dad.

Meanwhile, the death certificate arrived and I was able to apply for my dad's service record, which arrived that August. Over the next six months I was able to use this, together with Pete's blog, the O.R.B. for 1945 and my dad's log book, to write a comprehensive account of his training, his postings and the operations in which he took part. By this time I had become intrigued by the prospect of discovering just who my dad's comrades were and what had happened to their pilot, who had been replaced immediately after their last operation by Flight Lieutenant Eric Butler. The only clue to his sudden departure was my brother's vague recollection that it was something to do with the death of his brother.

With the help of the 'Wings over New Zealand Aviation Forum', I quickly discovered the tragic explanation and it turned out to be the first of many stories that illustrated the sacrifices made by the people of New Zealand during the Second World War. I had posted a question about Bill Mallon on the forum and within twenty four hours I had not only discovered the reason for Bill's disappearance but Chris Newey, whose uncle Gerry was a wireless operator with the squadron, had put me in touch

A page from Bob's log book showing five of his nine operations

with Bill's son Barrie, in Christchurch.

Barrie explained that both of Bill's brothers, Jack and Tom, were pilots and that Jack had been shot down and killed over France in 1940. Then, just a few days after Bill had started his operational tour with my dad in March 1945, he received news that his other brother, Tom, had also been killed after crashing his Mosquito in the Netherlands. Bill's family immediately started procedures to have him grounded but Bill continued his tour and the war was over before they succeeded.

My next discovery was what all historians long for, a first-hand account of the period they are researching. In 2004, at the age of 84, Bill had been interviewed by Martin Halliday as part of the New Zealand Defence Force 'Military Oral History Project'. In **June 2013** I acquired a copy of the transcript of this six hour conversation and it provides a fascinating insight into the challenges and opportunities faced by trainee pilots, particularly those from the other side of the world, but it also makes a valuable contribution to understanding life in New Zealand during the inter-war years.

In the interview Bill described how, as young boys, he and his brothers developed their passion for flying whilst watching Gypsy Moths at the local airfield on Sunday mornings. He also recalled how difficult life was in New Zealand during the Great Depression and was able to recount the details of his epic journey from New Zealand to England via the U.S.A. and Canada.

I also learnt of the life-long betrayal Bill felt over the refusal to recognize the part Jack played in the Battle of Britain and Barrie sent me copies of letters Bill had exchanged with the mayor of a small town near Calais where Jack is buried. I even discovered that most of the Mallon crew had made a trip to my home town in Lincolnshire in March 1945 to celebrate my dad's first wedding anniversary.

Things were now moving rapidly and in **July 2013** I received an amazing e-mail: '*Hi – our family has just found your blog – very interesting reading especially as my dad, Jim Haworth is mentioned. I have some information on the crew and their flights….. Would you be interested?*' It was from the navigator's eldest daughter Ruth, also in New Zealand, and '*interested*' doesn't begin to describe my feelings. Ruth's dad had written to her mum, Sally, throughout their long separation and she agreed to send me some of those letters.

As the only member of the crew with children, Jim clearly found absence from his wife and two little girls very difficult and, despite a wicked sense of humour and attempts to make light of a difficult situation, his homesickness permeated everything he wrote. I found Jim's letters very moving but very funny too and I was amazed by the amount of detail he included about their operations over Germany.

One of the highlights of **2013** occurred on the **1st August** when I received from New Zealand a signed copy of '*The Nazi and the Luftgangster*', a book co-written by Doug Williamson who was a flight engineer with the squadron. It tells the truly breath-taking story of how he literally fell out of his Lancaster and was captured by the Germans. After the war he emigrated to Canada, where he formed a life-long friendship with a young German with whom he co-wrote the book, and then to New Zealand where he now lives.

Later that month, I received another e-mail from New Zealand, this one from Keith Springer, a conservationist working to save threatened bird species on islands in the Antarctic, who had read my blog and been struck by a number of coincidences. His father, Randal Springer, was a wireless operator whose crew was posted to Mepal from No. 1669 H.C.U. on the same day as the Mallon crew and took part in several of the same operations. Randal was also at the Initial Training Wing (I.T.W.) in Rotorua at the same time as Bill Mallon and travelled to Canada in 1943, possibly on the same ship. Thankfully, his crew also survived the war.

The dedication in Doug's book, 2013

The Nazi
and the
Luftgangster

To Vic, whose Dad
Bob Jay who
Mentions my exploit in
his log book.. Dougie
D. B. Williamson
and 23/7/13
Lutz Dille

Throughout my research, I was on the lookout for

photographs of Lancasters with the identifying letters 'AA' or 'JN' that would signify they belonged to No. 75(NZ) Squadron. I found a few, some of them that could have been aircraft that my dad had flown in. I was dumbfounded in **October 2013** when I found a photograph in Simon's blog of Lancaster AA-W (RF127) that was taken, according to the caption, on the 24th April 1945 during a daylight operation to Bad Oldesloe in Germany. My dad's log book, the O.R.B. and Peter Wheeler of the New Zealand Bomber Command Association, all confirmed that this was the aircraft in which the Mallon crew was flying on this, their final war operation. I could even see my dad's head in the cockpit!

With that breakthrough and the completion of the chapters on Bill's brothers, I thought I had just about reached the end of the project and on the **9th February 2014** I e-mailed Simon to that effect:

Hi Simon,

I've written a post about Tom Mallon, the second of Bill's brothers to be killed, and although it's not about 75 I'm sure you will be interested. I think I'm coming to the end of my blog now, unless I discover anything about the remaining four crew members, but will probably do one last post about my dad's B.C. Clasp when it arrives.

Over the next few months, I was contacted by several other interested parties and any idea that I had come to the end of the project was being dispelled by the day. First of all, Evander Broekman e-mailed me about his work with a team from the Netherlands investigating servicemen reported 'missing in action'. He wanted to know more about Jack Mallon's crash and had some shocking photographs of the remains of a British aircraft shot down near Calais. It transpired that it was not Jack's aircraft but they were chilling nonetheless. Incredibly, nearly two years later, I did find a photograph of Jack's Blenheim shortly after it had crashed.

It was becoming clear to me that having made contact with the families of two of my dad's crew I was not going to rest until I had managed to trace the other four. I contacted the New Zealand Herald with a request to publish an appeal for information on the other two Kiwis in the crew, Ken Philp and Frank Symes. They were unable to help but Sarah Lawrance, the P.A. to its Editor in Chief, suggested I contact the New Zealand Woman's Weekly, which I did on the **11th March 2014**. I was rewarded for my efforts with an e-mail just three weeks later.

'*Hello. I am the daughter of Frank. Can I help in any way?*' It was from Yvonne Wairau, the daughter of wireless operator Frank Symes, and a few hours later her son Warren also e-mailed me. Warren later confirmed that a friend of Winnie, Frank's widow, had told her and Yvonne about my appeal in the Woman's Weekly and they were more than willing to help. I was soon able to complete yet another piece of this amazing jigsaw and Frank and Winnie's

Bob's Bomber Command clasp

twenty six grandchildren were a great boost to the blog's readership!

While I continued with my efforts to trace the rest of the crew, there were other interesting developments. I had tried to trace the mayor of Guînes, the small town near Calais where Jack Mallon is buried, to check the accuracy of what I had written about him. I had described him as '*a hero of the French resistance, who had made it his job to remind young people of the sacrifices made by Jack Mallon and his comrades*'. I eventually received a reply from his son who confirmed that everything I had said about his father was correct.

My dad's view of his medals was that they were an unwelcome reminder of a difficult period of history and they remained throughout his life in the original box at the back of a drawer, occasionally appearing when his children were bored. None of us was aware at the time of the simmering resentment felt by many veterans that the men who flew with Bomber Command had been conveniently forgotten by the government, an embarrassing reminder of their controversial strategy of 'Area Bombing.'

Following a review by Sir John Holmes into the awarding of military campaign medals it was announced on the 26th February 2013 by the Minister of State for Defence Personnel, Welfare and Veterans that there was at last to be a Bomber Command Clasp and that the applications process was open. I had a less jaundiced view than my dad of the awarding of honours to his generation and sent off my application immediately. I had to wait fifteen months, nothing compared to the almost seventy years that surviving veterans had had to wait, but on the **12th May 2014** the clasp arrived. It was a pity my dad couldn't have seen it.

In the **Summer of 2014**, I discovered the tragic fate of the R.A.F. pilot who had taken my dad up for his first three flights in December 1944. After a distinguished war record, Squadron Leader Alban Chipling D.F.C. was killed in a training accident in Gloucestershire. Nearly two years later, I was able to exchange e-mails with Antony, the great nephew of S/L Chipling, who obtained permission for me to publish some of his family's photographs.

So far, the year had seen a number of exciting developments in the story but the best was yet to come. On the **18th August 2014** I was able to walk in my dad's footsteps and board a Lancaster bomber, not just for a taxi run this time, but for a flight over the Lincolnshire countryside. It was difficult to describe the mixed emotions I felt as the majestic old warbird lifted off the tarmac of what

Bob's log book showing flights with S/L Chipling

was once R.A.F. Kirmington. The following day the International Bomber Command Centre agreed to feature Bob's story in its 'Memory Library'.

Then, just before **Christmas 2014**, Barrie Mallon sent me an image of a newspaper cutting from 'The Bay of Plenty Beacon' from March 1943. It announced the death of Hazel Waugh, the wife of my dad's replacement bomb aimer, Lance Waugh, just weeks after he had been posted overseas and more than two years before he would be able to return home again. The more I delved into the lives of the Mallon crew the more tragedies were being uncovered.

By this time, my attempts to trace the three remaining crew members were stalling, not helped by my own carelessness, having repeatedly misread the name of my dad's bomb aimer as Ken 'Philip' rather than 'Philp'. The fact that the rear gunner had been consistently referred to as 'John' or 'Johnny' Eynstone by both Bill Mallon and Jim Haworth, even though he was actually called Denis, didn't help either! In **November 2014** I had a breakthrough.

Geoff Swallow, an Australian involved in researching lost aircrew, had been following my dad's story on the blog and had found records of a Denis Eynstone who could be the gunner I was trying to trace, as well as possible names for his wife and daughter. Eynstone is not a common name and after some internet searches I posted a speculative letter to an address in Devon.

Just over a week later, I received a reply from Wendy, Denis's daughter. She confirmed that the address was correct, that Denis William Eynstone was her dad and that he had served with No. 75(NZ) Squadron. Unfortunately, he had died in 2011 at the age of eighty six but the new occupants of the house knew Wendy's address and were able to forward my letter. Wendy told me that Denis talked only occasionally about his wartime experiences and she was as puzzled as I was why he had been called John.

Despite her dad's reluctance to talk about his experiences, Wendy was able to provide me with lots of pictures and stories about him but the material she sent raised more questions than it answered. It wasn't until she obtained his service record that things became a lot clearer for us both. Wendy had no idea, for example, that her dad had re-enlisted several years after the war and served with a number of squadrons well into the 1950s.

It was at about this time that the penny finally

Ken Philp's memorial plaque (picture: Glen Turner)

dropped and I realized that the name of the bomb aimer was Philp and not Philip. With the help of Glen Turner of the 75 Squadron Association (N.Z.) and Warren Wairau I managed to discover that Ken Philp had died in 1991 and was buried in the Whenua Tapu Cemetery in Pukerua Bay, Porirua. It was another four months, in **March 2015**, before Warren e-mailed me with the thrilling news that he was in touch with Allan, Ken's nephew, who had a telephone number for Ken's son David. I had to wait until July before I finally received information about Ken and I learnt of yet another family tragedy. Bill wasn't the only member of the crew to have had a brother shot down and killed in France.

In **December 2015**, I received a request from Michel Beckers in the Netherlands who was compiling memorials for 'fallen heroes' on the 'Aircrew Remembered' website. He was seeking permission to use material from my blog to create a memorial for Jack Mallon and in return he provided me with an extraordinary photograph. There are now memorials for both Jack and Tom on the website and I have a photograph of the aircraft in which Jack Mallon was fatally wounded, being guarded by two German soldier just hours after it crashed.

There is now just one remaining crew member to trace, Don Cook, the mid-upper gunner. After four years, I am nowhere nearer making a breakthrough and with a surname that is fairly common a number of false trails have ended in disappointment. All that is known about him is that he was twenty years of age and possibly from the London area. At the time of writing, I am still trying to locate Don's family or, who knows, maybe even Don himself.

Up to the present day, surprises are continuing to keep me enthralled. On the **1st March 2016** I received an e-mail informing me that one of the men who flew with the Mallon crew as mid-under gunner on three operations, Charles Green, is still very much alive. I never dreamt my research would culminate in my having the opportunity to have a long conversation with a man who shared with my dad the cramped space inside a Lancaster more than seventy years earlier.

Sadly, the rest of the Mallon crew had died by the time I embarked on this project but writing this book, seventy years after the war, has given their families the opportunity to learn more about their experiences. It has also enabled me to get that bit closer to my dad, who missed most of the milestones in my adult life.

2 HOPES FOR A BRIGHTER FUTURE

Left to right top: Bob, Phyllis and Fred Jay junior in Great Yarmouth, 1922

It was April 1919 and Sarah Jay had every reason to be hopeful about her family's future. She had just given birth to her third child, a beautiful baby boy, and her husband Fred was about to be discharged from the army. The Great War, 'the war to end all wars', was soon to end officially with the signing of the Treaty of Versailles and two British aviators, John Alcock and Arthur Brown, were preparing to embark on their historic transatlantic flight. Sarah, of course, would have been unaware of that and it would be many years before anyone in the family would realise its significance.

Sarah was desperate for a family life more fulfilling than the one that she and her mother had known. Born to an unmarried eighteen year old in 1886, she was fully aware of the stigma attached to her illegitimacy and was determined to give her children what she had never had. Her mother had died three years earlier in the hospital that had been the workhouse in Great Yarmouth and she had never known her father.

Before the war she had worked in a silk factory in Great Yarmouth and Fred had trained as a cobbler and boot maker. Shortly after they married, on Boxing Day 1912, they moved to the thriving fishing port of Grimsby where, in February 1914, their first child, Phyllis Mary, was born

The family moved again in 1915, this time to Leicester, where Fred acquired valuable additional skills working as a 'leather stitcher' at the Cooperative Boot and Shoe Factory in the city. The factory, opened in 1887, was thriving at this time making boots for the army as well as continuing to produce high quality civilian footwear. He enlisted in December 1915 and, a few months later, Sarah gave birth to their second child, a boy they named Fred. With two children and a husband in the army Sarah returned to Grimsby.

Fred senior was judged unfit for trench warfare and was eventually attached to the First Leicestershire 'Home Service Garrison Battalion'. He spent the latter part of his four years' service guarding German prisoners of war and burying the dead in Ypres and Arras and it was only in later life when I visited the war graves and memorials in Belgium and France that I fully understood why he was so reluctant to talk about his experiences.

One of Fred's souvenirs, a painting of the Hotel de Ville in Arras

Among the souvenirs he brought home were a model tank, crafted out of brass by German prisoners, and two three inch diameter artillery shells. One of these had the words *'Leicestershires, Pte F. Jay, France 1914 1919'* beaten into its surface, the other *'Souvenier of the war, 1914 1919'* and both have ornate floral designs. In

Arras he purchased from a local artist a painting of the burning Hotel de Ville in the city's Place des Héros, an iconic image that still hangs on the wall in our home in North Yorkshire.

A personal highlight for me in 2015 was a 'pilgrimage' to France and Belgium, where I was able to walk in my grandad's footsteps through Ypres, Arras and Albert almost one hundred years after he had carried out his gruesome tasks. Another, in August of that year, was even more memorable when I was able to walk in my dad's footsteps, or should that be 'fly in his slipstream', and take part in a thirty minute flight in a Lancaster bomber over the barely recognisable airfields of my home county of Lincolnshire, 'Bomber County'.

Private Fred Jay, 1916

When Fred was demobbed at the end of 1919, the couple settled in the New Clee area of Grimsby with their young family; Phyllis, who was nearly six, Fred junior, nearly four, and their new baby boy. Fred quickly established himself as a highly skilled boot and shoe maker and was able to set up his own business with a small cobbler's shop on the corner of Rutland Street, just around the corner from their home in Spencer Street, now the site of a supermarket.

They had christened their baby Robert, after Fred's father, and Bob, as he became known, was soon playing happily with his older sister and brother and enjoying family holidays with his grandparents, uncles and aunts in Great Yarmouth. None of them could have imagined that just twenty years later a war even more apocalyptic than the one that had just ended would once again engulf the world, be responsible for the deaths of more than fifty million people and have a lasting impact on their family.

Eleven thousand miles away, and almost exactly a year after Bob was born, in the small town of Bell Block in Taranaki, on the North Island of New Zealand, twins Bill and Dora May were born, completing the family of Alexander (Alec) and Dora Mallon. Like Fred, Alec had moved from his home town in search of work, in his case from Australia, and, like Fred, he also had two older children, Tom and Jack, born in 1914 and 1916, the same years as Phyllis and Fred Jay junior.

Born in 1876, Alec was ten years older than Fred and his military service had been with the New South Wales Mounted Rifles in the Boer War (1899 – 1902) rather than the 'Great War'. He had left Australia in 1910, arriving in New Zealand a couple of years before Fred arrived in Grimsby. His first job there was on the building of the breakwater for the port of New Plymouth, after which he was employed by Inglewood and

The New South Wales Mounted Rifles, 1900. (picture courtesy of National Boer War Memorial Association, Australia)

then Taranaki County Councils as a road maintenance worker, a job he stuck with for most of his working life.

Alec and Dora had married in 1912, the same year as Fred and Sarah, and settled in Bell Block where they had a house built, which is still standing today, and where their two sons were born. After the war Dora became pregnant again and no parents could have been prouder when their twins were born on the 9th April 1920. Their hopes for the future were every bit as optimistic as those of Fred and Sarah.

Bob attended St. John the Evangelist Church School on

St John's School, 1931. Bob is centre, front row

Cleethorpes Road, Grimsby, from the age of five but he was happiest playing in the streets and swimming, when the weather and tides permitted, in the murky waters of the River Humber. All year, throughout the 1920s, he looked forward to the family holidays in Great Yarmouth where, in the 1950s, the second period of post-war austerity of the century, we had the same holidays, stayed in the same house and played on the same beach as my dad, thirty years earlier.

Bill attended Bell Block Primary School and lived more of a rural life than Bob, carrying out odd jobs on the land and fishing or swimming when he was not at school. He remembered some of the children arriving at school with no shoes and some, from outlying areas, on horseback. Their house wasn't connected up to an electricity supply until about 1925 and had no sewerage system but the Mallons always considered themselves to be very fortunate, particularly when the 'Great Depression' hit New Zealand. Alec always had a job and the house had a large garden and, as Bill explained in the interview he gave in 2004,

Dad was a good gardener. We lived off the garden as far as vegetables and those sort of things. Plus he had little bit of extra land where he grew enough potatoes for the family for the year so there was no such thing as having to purchase potatoes or anything like that.

Others in the neighbourhood weren't as fortunate. Bill remembered his dad giving away vegetables to relatives and getting upset at the impact of unemployment on some of the men.

My father was put in charge of gangs for the Council and he used to have... the unemployed coming out from New Plymouth to do their half a day, one day or a day and half's work, depending on the size of their families... it was called the dole in those days. They had to work for the dole and they'd come out to the pits and work out there. It used to upset him sometimes you know, he'd have men out there who were lawyers, accountants and those sorts of things - had never worked manually in their lives and then suddenly confronted with having to crack stones in a quarry to be able to get enough money to take care of their families. He used to be quite upset about these men having to virtually beg for their dole.

Dora and Bill Mallon, 1924

Bob left school shortly after his fourteenth birthday, in April 1933 and started a seven year apprenticeship with Grimsby Motors, still wearing short trousers under his overalls. Always an active boy, he and a friend had cycled from Grimsby to Great Yarmouth the previous summer, a distance of one hundred and forty four miles, sleeping for one night in the open air.

He joined a boxing club in 1934, at about the same time that Max Baer defeated the huge Primo Carnera to become Heavyweight Champion of the World, not just to keep fit but to pursue what he considered the 'Noble Art'.

He enjoyed some minor success until one day, after a fighter withdrew, he was asked at short notice to take part in a bout in a 'gentlemen's club'. He found the atmosphere of beer, smoke and the baying for blood overwhelming and after three rounds of what he later described as 'Hell on Earth' he decided it wasn't the career for him.

The New Clee Boxing Club, 1935. Bob is on the right, middle row

Fred's cobbler's shop wasn't the first of its kind to be a hot bed of socialism and Bob formed his political ideals listening to Fred and his friends putting the world to rights and arguing about the socialist credentials of the Soviet Union. He was an avid reader of political books and pamphlets and the novels of writers such as Jack London, Upton Sinclair and Robert Tressell.

At the age of thirteen, Bill left Bell Block School and went on to New Plymouth Boys' High School where he threw himself into all aspects of school life. He joined the Army Cadet Corps, something that he spoke very positively about in later life, particularly the opportunities it gave to students to take responsibility and develop feelings of comradeship. Anzac Days were particularly memorable for Bill when the whole school would march to the New Plymouth cenotaph and on to Pukekura Park where a remembrance service was held. These services would take on added poignancy for Bill and his family after the war.

A Labour government was elected in New Zealand for the first time in 1935, under the leadership of Michael Savage, but, unlike the Jays,

New Plymouth Boys' High School 1st XI, 1935. Bill is second left, middle row

the Mallon family were not particularly interested in politics. Being from a farming community they were suspicious of what a Labour government would mean for their way of life, more out of concern for the threat of the unknown than of any political conviction.

After six years, Bob was released early from his apprenticeship as a fully qualified motor mechanic and, in April 1939, shortly after his 20th birthday, he joined the local fire brigade. Five months later, at 11.15 a.m. on the 3rd September 1939, Bob and his family sat around the radio and listened with horror as Prime Minister Neville Chamberlain made an announcement. Germany had failed to give an undertaking to withdraw troops from Poland and *'consequently this country is at war ...'* As the father of two young men and after what he had seen in France and Belgium one can only imagine Fred's feelings on hearing that announcement.

Since they were small boys, Bill and his brothers had been going to Bell Block airfield every Sunday to watch Gipsy Moths taking off and landing and a fascination with flying had developed in all three of them. John, or Jack as he was known, was particularly keen, Bill later describing him as being *'very air minded'*, so much so that he joined the local aero club in 1936.

A DH60G Gipsy Moth (picture: Alan Eggeling via S.A. Airways Museum Society)

In 1938, Jack joined the Civil Reserve as a pilot and received his initial flying instruction with the Western Federated Aero Club in Bell Block. Bill remembers young men paying ten shillings for fifteen minutes in the air but Jack's training was subsidised by the government and he soon obtained his 'A' Endorsed Licence. He then applied successfully for a commission in the R.A.F. and left for England in June 1939.

Bill had left school at the end of 1936 having turned sixteen and, although he had not managed to pass the School Certificate, his education had progressed considerably further than Bob's. He had acquired a good background in engineering at the High School and started work in February 1937 at Newton King Ltd. in the motor spares department. In 1939, the same year in which Bob joined the Fire Brigade, Bill became a volunteer fire fighter.

Mussolini's invasion of Ethiopia in 1935 and Hitler's annexation of Austria in 1938 had contributed to a growing sense of unease in New Zealand as well as in Britain and, although the political implications may not have been fully understood, Bill's parents and the rest of their generation knew enough to be very concerned. Bill later confirmed that they were *'greatly saddened by the situation'*. On the 3rd September 1939, at

Bill, in the passenger seat of a New Plymouth Fire Brigade Bedford hose tender, shortly after becoming a volunteer fire fighter in 1939. Bill sent this picture to Jack, in England – it was returned with the rest of his belongings in 1940

11.30 p.m. New Zealand Standard Time, a couple of hours later than Chamberlin's broadcast in Britain, the Mallon family listened to acting Prime Minister Peter Fraser declaring that New Zealand also was at war with Germany.

Their sense of dread was probably even greater than that felt in the Jay household at that time as Jack, who had been accepted for a short service commission in the R.A.F., was already in England with No. 53 Squadron and Tom, who was managing his own shop at Moturoa, was a member of the Wellington West Coast Territorial Army unit.

Bill recalled that his father was '*very upset*' about the outbreak of war and that his mother was reluctant to talk about it. They had every reason to worry – by the time the war was over they would have lost two of their four children.

In June of that year, along with all young men of his age, Bob had had to register at the local Ministry of Labour office under the terms of the Military Training Act (1939). This act, passed on the 26th May in the face of imminent conflict in Europe, required all men born between 4th June 1918 and 3rd June 1919 to register, after which they would be called up for six month's full-time military training and then transferred to the Reserve.

To ensure that the call up did not take men away from vital industries and services, as had happened during the 'Great War', the Government introduced a '*Schedule of Reserved Occupations*', which meant that men meeting the age criteria laid out in the schedule were '*reserved in their present occupation*'. Reserved occupations included engineers, dockers and merchant seaman and, as a full-time fireman, Bob met the criteria in the schedule and remained in the fire service.

Bob (front) with fellow firemen in 1940

Being politically aware, Bob understood the threat posed by fascism and had followed closely the rise of Hitler in Germany, the progress of the Spanish Civil War and Mussolini's actions in Abyssinia. The so-called 'Phoney War', the period of relative inaction following the declaration of war, was short-lived and as the fighting spread across the world it was inevitable that he would have to play his part at some time. What he didn't know at that time was that he would soon go from fire fighter to fire starter!

With one brother in the R.A.F. and a keen interest in aviation, both Bill and Tom were determined that they too would become pilots and '*do their bit*' for their country. It would become a source of great frustration for Bill that it would be more than five years before he could commence operational flying and he could never have anticipated the tragic circumstances that would bring it to an abrupt end.

3 BOB JAY: THE PERILS OF 'SCRUMPY'

Sgt Bob Jay, November 1944

By 1942, German troops had advanced as far as Stalingrad, the mass murder of Jews and other groups across Europe was well under way and the Japanese were overwhelming large areas in the Far East. There was wide-spread support for Stalin's call for the opening of a 'Second Front' to relieve pressure on the Soviet Union and Bob probably saw joining the air force as his contribution to this campaign. I'm sure his decision had nothing to do with the destruction of his dad's cobbler's shop in an air raid in 1940!

Bob volunteered to join the Royal Air Force Volunteer Reserve (R.A.F.V.R.) and was instructed to attend R.A.F. Padgate, near Warrington, on the **30th September 1942**, where he was assessed and interviewed by No. 10 Aviation Candidate Selection Board (A.C.S.B.) His service record shows that at the end of the process he was *'Not recommended for aircrew duties'*, a decision generally made for *'aptitude, educational or medical'* reasons, and it was a huge disappointment to Bob who had dreamt of flying and hitting back at Nazi Germany. The reason for the recommendation was not stated.

At this stage, the majority of pilots, navigators and bomb aimers were being drawn from ex-grammar school and university volunteers and Bob did talk about being handicapped by leaving school at fourteen with a lack of mathematical skills. This may or may not have been the reason for his rejection on this occasion but, if it were, it would go a long way towards explaining why he was so desperate for his children to do well at school and why both our parents made such enormous sacrifices to enable all three of us to take our education as far as possible.

Disappointed but undeterred, he returned to Grimsby and his job as a fireman, in what in August the previous year had become the National Fire Service, and he reapplied to the R.A.F. ten months later. On the **28th July 1943**, he was instructed to attend No. 1 A.C.S.B. at R.A.F. Doncaster where he was once again assessed and interviewed. He was more successful second time around and *'recommended for training as a Flight Engineer'*, a role that at the time was in great demand because of the introduction of the four engine Stirling and Lancaster bombers. With excitement and some trepidation he returned home to await further instructions and continued with the most challenging period of his career so far.

During the months of June and July 1943, nearly one hundred and fifty residents of Grimsby and Cleethorpes were killed in air raids, ninety nine of them on one night in June. Bob and his colleagues were stretched to breaking point as they were called to deal with the aftermath of high explosives, incendiary devices and, on the night of 14th June, hundreds of a new type of anti-personnel bomb, the 'butterfly bomb'.

Two key features made these new bombs so deadly. First, they had rotating wings to slow their fall and act as hooks to hang on trees and gutters and second, they could be armed with one of three fuses, the impact fuse, delay fuse and anti-disturbance fuse. When deployed together in a precise and methodical order, such as in the Grimsby and Cleethorpes raids, they caused the maximum amount of terror, chaos and death.

Air raids on Bob's home town became much less frequent after the summer of 1943 as the Luftwaffe's attention was diverted further east and, on the **2nd September 1943**, Bob was ordered once more to attend R.A.F. Doncaster, this time for a two day assessment, including a medical that he passed with

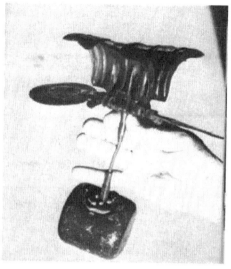

A butterfly bomb (picture: David Thornton)

medical category grade 1'. He was officially enlisted 'D.P.E.', for the 'Duration of the Present Emergency', and was mustered as 'Aircraft hand/Flight Engineer' ('ACH/F.Eng') with the rank of Aircraftsman Second Class (A.C.2) grade A, the starting grade.

Having sworn his allegiance to King and Country, he was issued with service number 1596172, placed on reserve and once again instructed to go home and wait. Two weeks later he received a letter from the Air Ministry welcoming him into the R.A.F. and advising him on preparations for his air force career. The letter also had a rather convoluted explanation for the delay in commencing training:

The Royal Air Force is a highly organised service. In the first line are trained and experienced crews whose stirring deeds and indomitable courage daily provoke the admiration of the world. Behind these men, ready to give them immediate support, are the newly-trained crews fresh from the schools. In your turn you and other accepted candidates stand ready to fill the schools. Without you, time might be lost at a critical moment in filling up the training facilities left vacant by those who have joined the ranks of the first line combatants, and the vital flow of reinforcements would be broken. Vacancies may also be caused by increased training requirements, for the schools are being rapidly expanded. For these reasons we must have a reserve of selected candidates like you on whom to call.

The letter concluded with what can only be described as a rallying cry:

In wishing you success in the Service of your choice I would like to add this: the Honour of the Royal Air Force is in your hands. Our country's safety and the final overthrow of the powers of evil now arrayed against us depend upon you and your comrades. You will be given the best aircraft and armament that the factories of Britain and America can produce. Equip yourself with knowledge of how to use them.

Good luck!

Archibald Sinclair - SECRETARY OF STATE FOR AIR.

Bob's call-up came in the New Year and, on the **17th January 1944**, he reported for five weeks basic training at No.3 Aircrew Receiving Centre (A.C.R.C.) at R.A.F. Regent's Park in London.

In the first few days, he was given a regulation haircut, a thorough dental check and inoculations against diphtheria, typhoid and small pox. The dental inspection had a rather unfortunate outcome as the accepted wisdom in R.A.F. dentistry was that any 'problem' teeth should be removed before any high altitude flying was undertaken. Pain caused by pressure changes, known as barodontalgia, or aerodontalgia in a purely aviation context, was too great a risk in combat and Bob had all of his top teeth and several bottom teeth removed.

As well as his new dentures, he received all his basic R.A.F. kit and 'Service Dress' uniform, commonly referred to as 'Best Blues', including the white cap insert that identified him as trainee aircrew, clearly visible three months later on his wedding pictures. He was instructed to mark every item of kit with his service number and expected to keep every item spotlessly clean in readiness for regular inspections.

The piece of kit that would have been the starkest reminder of the perilous nature of the task ahead was his pair of identity discs. Manufactured from fire-resistant material and with the airman's religion clearly punched between his service number and name, none of the recruits could have been in any doubt why they had to wear these when they were flying.

Over the next few weeks, he faced a rigorous daily routine of fatigues, inspections, training drills, lectures and assessments, a routine that Bob would have found rather challenging having left school nearly eleven years earlier. As an A.C.2

One of Bob's identity discs

grade A, his pay of three shillings a day plus sixpence a day war pay, which he collected at the fortnightly pay parade, was considerably less than his pay as a fireman but at least he didn't have to pay for his food and accommodation - not that the food was particularly appetising.

At meal times, an officer always asked if there were any complaints about the food. The young airmen learned quickly that it was a good idea to say nothing, as anyone who did complain might be faced with peeling vast quantities of potatoes or scrubbing dozens of encrusted pots and pans. Bob was no exception, until the day they served up rancid herrings, boiled, un-gutted and with their heads on and he decided enough was enough. When the officer made the usual bored request Bob stood up and said *'Yes sir, I have a complaint.'* Apparently, you could have heard a pin drop as the officer walked the length of the mess to confront Bob, demanding to know the nature of his complaint.

'It's the fish.' said Bob.

'And what's wrong with the fish?' came the reply *'There are people in civvy street who would give their back teeth to be able to eat fresh fish.'*

'Well, for a start it's not fresh. It's not prepared properly and it's not cooked properly. In fact, it's inedible.'

Albert Stephenson, trawler skipper, 1919

The irate officer demanded to know what qualified Bob to pass judgement on the cooking abilities of the catering staff and how he knew so much about fish. *'I'm from Grimsby,'* he said, and went on to tell the officer that everyone in Grimsby knew about fish. In his own family his grandfather, also called Robert Jay, had been a fisherman and then a fish hawker in Great Yarmouth, his brother Fred had worked on the fish docks in Grimsby since leaving school and his future father-in-law, Albert Stephenson, had been a trawler skipper sailing out of Grimsby since the First World War. The officer had all the fish sent back to the kitchens where it was thrown in the 'swill bin' to become food for the local pigs.

By the end of **February 1944**, Bob had completed this first stage of his training and was posted to No. 7 Initial Training Wing (I.T.W.) at R.A.F. Newquay, in Cornwall. There, according to the pamphlet *'You are going to be a Flight Engineer'*, handed to all those trainees destined to take on that role, the R.A.F. would *'lay a foundation of discipline, physical fitness and mental alertness'* and provide a *'sound basic knowledge of the R.A.F.'* He was also issued with his 'War Service uniform', or 'battledress', and later on in the course with flying clothing which included his helmet, with oxygen and communication mask, goggles, flying suit, Mae West life jacket and parachute harness.

The I.T.W. syllabus included such things as aircraft recognition, air reconnaissance, meteorology and the principles of flight. The one surviving exercise book from Bob's time at the I.T.W. consists of just thirty eight pages and contains brief notes on Morse code, aeronautical terminology and several pages of mathematical calculations.

There was clearly very little time to go into much depth with his studies and the mathematics was quite basic, although probably not for someone who had left school at the age of fourteen. There had obviously been some effort to make the problem-solving relevant, with problems involving the calculation of air speed at different altitudes, the relationship between bomb load, air speed, altitude and fuel consumption and the effect on the balance of the aircraft of crew members moving fore and aft.

There are also dimensions, descriptions and diagrams to assist in the recognition of Allied and enemy aircraft, notes on the Sten gun and the .38 Smith and Wesson handgun, and nine sides of closely written notes on the Browning .303 machine gun. Bob and his fellow trainees were expected to undertake some basic firearms training, which proved to be almost as dangerous as his encounters with the enemy a year later.

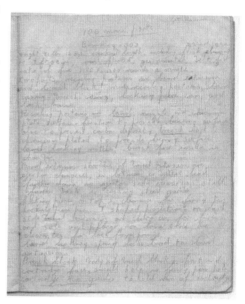

The Sten gun was a British-made sub-machine gun that could be produced cheaply, quickly and in great numbers. First dreamed up in the opening months of the war and then rushed into production in 1940, the Sten weighed three-kilograms, was all-metal and fired eight rounds a second from a horizontally-loaded, 32-round magazine. Each one cost as little as £2 to produce, roughly equal to about £80 today, and nearly five million

Some of Bob's notes on the .303 machine gun

were manufactured before the end of 1945, the weapon going on to serve in every theatre of war.

Unfortunately, early versions were notoriously unreliable and had two annoying habits: jamming and not firing at all or firing uncontrollably in full automatic mode when '*dropped, jostled or even just set down carelessly*' (See 'The Venerable Sten - The Allies' 10 Dollar Submachine Gun'). British troops had allegedly learnt to use this second shortcoming to their advantage during urban combat by simply tossing one or two loaded and

Bob, 3rd from left, middle row, with fellow trainees

cocked Stens through a door or window, whereupon they could fire the whole magazine in all directions.

Bob and his fellow trainees commenced their firearms training on a firing range backed by a rocky outcrop or cliff. The instructor told them that the Sten could be set to fire single shots, bursts or even to fire off the whole magazine, this last setting being one they were not to use, for reasons of economy or safety, he didn't specify which. One by one, the men took the machine gun and fired single shots and one burst each at a target against the rocks.

One particularly nervous chap took the weapon and squeezed the trigger. As it began to fire he panicked and dropped it to the ground, where it continued firing in automatic mode and started to spin, firing bullets in all directions. Several of his comrades had to jump wildly into the air as the muzzle of the gun spun towards them before the instructor avoided a tragedy by seizing the weapon and discharging it into the ground.

As if firing a Sten gun wasn't hazardous enough, the next stage in their weapons training was learning how to throw a hand grenade. The trainees had to practise using an overarm bowling action to throw a wooden dummy grenade between two posts and over the bar of a structure similar to rugby posts. After a number of attempts all but one of the men had managed to score a 'try'. One young man, however, just couldn't get the hang of it. He repeatedly released the grenade too soon, which sent it high into the air, landing only a few yards away. After a lot of practice he eventually managed to achieve a couple of throws where the grenade followed the correct trajectory. The session was to finish with each trainee throwing one live grenade but, as so much time had been taken to get them all up to the required standard, they were told to come back the next day to do their 'live' throws.

There was to be a parade, or some other formal occasion, the following day so they all turned up bright and early in their 'best blues'. In turn they took their 'live' throws without incident, bending low behind a pile of sandbags as each grenade exploded. The young man who had struggled the previous day confidently took his grenade, adopted the correct stance, pulled the pin and launched the grenade - almost vertically high into the air. It landed just a few yards the other side of the sandbags. Almost as one, the instructor and the trainees threw themselves flat on their faces in the mud. The grenade exploded with an ear-splitting bang, some of the sandbags disintegrated and everyone was showered with mud, sand and grass. Bob didn't say if they managed to clean themselves up in time for the parade.

Bob & Vera's wedding, 19th April 1944

Trainees were assessed throughout the I.T.W. course and had to pass a series of examinations before any further posting. Bob was relieved to get over this hurdle and, after a week's attachment at R.A.F. Wrexham, was granted three days leave to travel home to Grimsby to negotiate another. He was getting married.

His wedding to Vera, the daughter of Albert and Ada Stephenson, took place in rather unusual circumstances. Vera was still only nineteen and needed her father's blessing to marry but there had been some problems within the family.

Albert was refusing to sanction the wedding, so permission was sought from a local magistrate. Wearing his R.A.F. uniform and speaking in his usual confident way, Bob had little difficulty persuading the magistrate that he was a fine upstanding young man worthy of anyone's hand in marriage. The magistrate then directed some harsh words at Albert, pointing out that his own service record as the skipper of an Armed Trawler during World War One, should have given him more sense.

The wedding took place in St James Church, now Grimsby Minster, on the **19th April 1944**, less than a year after it had been badly damaged by a German bomb. Vera had a milk round and her colleagues

St James Church after the air raid on the 13th July 1943 (picture courtesy of Grimsby Evening Telegraph)

from the dairy provided a 'guard of honour' with milk bottles for the happy couple as they left the church.

Bob's next posting was to No.5 School of Technical Training (S.o.T.T.) at R.A.F. Locking near Weston-super-Mare, Somerset in **May 1944**, where he carried out the first phase of his 'trade' training as a Flight Engineer. This phase consisted of ten weeks of 'preliminary' training on airframes, engines, carburettors, electrics, instruments, hydraulics and propellers.

Distances between locations on the Locking base were considerable, so Bob had his bicycle sent to him by rail. Most of the trainees appear to have had little respect for the notion of private property and the first one out of the hut would grab the first bike he could find and pedal off, so Bob's was constantly disappearing and then reappearing a day or two later. The notion of 'community cycles' appears to have been very popular in the R.A.F. long before 'Boris bikes' were thought of in London, and despite Bob's socialist beliefs he found this very frustrating.

'Guard of honour' at Bob & Vera's wedding

During his limited leave, Bob found the perils of 'Scrumpy', the local Somerset brew, every bit as challenging as the training. The 'Urban Dictionary' describes 'Scrumpy' as

Surprisingly refreshing and can be consumed in vast quantities providing the drinker does not want to use his legs for the next five hours!

And, if Bob had been aware of this, he might have been a little more circumspect before downing several pints of the stuff in a local pub before attempting to cycle back to the base. He set off with a mate on the cross bar and, within a few hundred yards and in the total darkness of the blackout, rode straight into a twelve foot deep irrigation ditch.

They survived but Bob's problems didn't end there. In their hut, the trainees were regularly waking up to find the inside of one of their boots soaking wet, the product of what became known as 'the phantom pisser'. Several of them had suffered, including Bob, and it became clear that one of them, probably under the influence of 'Scrumpy', was using a boot from under the bed as a chamber pot. No-one was more disgusted by this antic than Bob, brought up as he was to know right from wrong and to respect his comrades.

Unfortunately, Bob had also grown up in a home without an inside toilet, always relying on a 'gazunder' for nocturnal urination, and to his horror and shame he eventually discovered that **he** was the mysterious boot-filler.

On the **12th July 1944**, he was posted to No. 4 S.o.T.T. at R.A.F. St. Athan, in South Wales, to complete the second and third phases of his flight engineer training. Phase 2 consisted of seven weeks of 'intermediate' training and, having completed this phase, Bob was reclassified on the 1st of September as Aircraftsman Second Class (AC2) grade B. His pay would have increased from three shillings a day to five shillings a day.

The final phase consisted of seven weeks of 'advanced' training on a specific aircraft and usually included a week at the factory of an aircraft manufacturer, a so-called 'Makers Course', but there is no record of this in Bob's service record. This was followed by a week of written and oral exams.

Flight Engineer's brevet

Having successfully completed the course and passed his exams, Bob attended a 'passing out' parade on the **13th November 1944**, where he was presented with his Flight Engineer's brevet and promoted to the rank of Sergeant, the minimum rank for aircrew. His pay was increased to twelve shillings a day but, had he achieved a mark of 70% or more in the exams, he would have been considered for a commission and even higher pay. His mark was 66.1%.

On the **25th November 1944**, Bob started the final stage of his training when he was posted, along with a number of other flight engineers, to No. 1669 Heavy Conversion Unit (H.C.U.) at R.A.F. Langar on the Nottinghamshire Leicestershire border. Although he was qualified as a Flight Engineer, he had not put any of his training into practice and was yet to fly. Within three weeks he would have his first taste of flying before joining the Mallon crew.

His log book records his first three flights, a total of nine hours in the air, in a Lancaster bomber on the 17th, 18th and 21st of December 1944 with Squadron Leader Alban Chipling D.F.C., an experienced pilot with an impressive war record. They carried out a number of circuits and landings, or 'circuits and bumps' as they were affectionately known, and some three engine landings, practice that was to prove crucial to the Mallon crew's survival on one of their operations a few months later.

Despite his vast experience, S/L Chipling became yet another tragic link to the Mallon crew when, three months later and just two weeks before V.E. Day, he was killed in a flying accident. The successful completion of war operations clearly did not mean that danger was over, particularly at a time when aviation was still at a relatively primitive stage.

S/L Chipling D.F.C. (picture: Sandra Stutely)

Alban Philip Sidney Chipling was born in December, 1913, the son of Sydney and Ella Chipling, in Grindleford, near Bakewell in Derbyshire. He had three older sisters, Grace, Sybil and Elfrida and was educated at Bracondale School in Norwich. He joined the R.A.F.V.R. in 1938, eventually serving with No. 429 Squadron R.C.A.F.

In the spring of 1939, as war loomed in Europe, he married Kathleen Marie Fitzgerald in her home town of Cambridge and received his commission to the rank of Pilot Officer on 30th September 1941. He was promoted to Flying Officer exactly one year later. He had a near miss on an operation to bomb Essen on the night of 12th/13th March 1943, when his aircraft was slightly damaged by flak but he and his crew brought the aircraft safely back to the U.K. and landed at R.A.F. East Moor, near York, at 0020hrs.

He was promoted to the rank of Flight Lieutenant on 17th July 1943 and awarded the D.F.C. on the 7th December of that year, his citation stating that he had 'completed many successful operations against the enemy in which he ... displayed high skill, fortitude and devotion to duty'.

By the end of 1944, he was instructing aircrew at 1669 HCU, where Bob met him, and was subsequently transferred to the Empire Central Flying School (E.C.F.S.) at R.A.F. Hullavington, near Chippenham in Wiltshire. On the morning of the 23rd April 1945 North American Harvard IIB FT232 took off from R.A.F. Hullavington with S/L Chipling flying second pilot to S/L James Russell Johnson A.F.C.

At approximately 1200 the aircraft failed to recover from a spin and, probably as a result of the pilot over-correcting, it crashed into the ground at Southrop, Gloucestershire. The cause of the accident was subsequently attributed to the failure to remove the ballast weights that should only be carried during solo flights.

Squadron Leaders Chipling and Johnson were laid to rest in the London Road cemetery in Chippenham on the 25th April 1945 with full military honours. His widow, Kathleen, who never re-married, died in Cambridge in 1996 at the age of 85.

Another illustration of the power of the internet was my discovery of several photographs of the two pilots' funeral on the website of ancestry.co.uk and the subsequent exchange of e-mails with Alban's great nephew, Antony, who had posted them several years earlier. Antony is the grandson of Alban's middle sister, Sybil, and Sandra Stutely, who owns the pictures, is the daughter of his youngest sister, Elfrida.

As Bob embarked on the final months of his war service, he would always remember the pilot who had first shown him what it was like to fly in a Lancaster, but he would live the rest of his life unaware of the tragedy that befell him.

*The funeral of S/L Chipling and S/L Johnson in Chippenham on the 25th April 1945
(picture: Sandra Stutely via ancestry.co.uk)*

4 BILL MALLON: AN EPIC JOURNEY

Sgt (later F/S) Bill Mallon, November 1943

The outbreak of war in **September 1939** brought uncertainty to the motor trade in New Zealand, as it did across the world, with doubts over the imports of new vehicles, the expected increase in fuel prices and the diversion of spare parts manufacture to the war effort. The boss at Newton King invited Bill into his office and explained the situation, suggesting that he could avoid redundancy by taking up a job at John Avery Ltd, a related business trading in 'fancy goods', toiletries and chocolate. It was not the area in which Bill had anticipated he would work but he accepted the offer, certain that it would only be a temporary position.

In **July 1940**, Bill received a letter that would prove to be the last he would ever hear from his brother Jack. Writing from his squadron's new home at R.A.F. Detling in the south of England, he wanted to know all about the sinking of the Niagara, an event that had brought the war so much closer to the shores of New Zealand. R.M.S. Niagara was an ocean liner owned by the Union Steam Ship Company and, rather unfortunately, originally nicknamed 'the Titanic of the Pacific'.

Shortly after leaving Auckland harbour on the 19th June 1940, it had struck a mine laid by the German auxiliary cruiser Orion and

R.M.S. Niagara (picture: Keith Gordon)

sank. No lives were lost but a huge consignment of gold, payment from the U.K. to the U.S.A. for munitions supplies, went down with the ship. Most of it was salvaged the following year and another thirty gold bars in 1953. It is believed there are a few still on the sea bed.

In **October 1940**, not long after Bill had posted his reply to his brother and while working as a salesman for John Avery, he received the devastating news that Jack had been shot down and was missing in France. It was subsequently confirmed that he had died as a result of his injuries, although it was many years before the family learned the details of his death. Bill and his brother Tom had already volunteered to join the air force by this time and the news only made them all the more determined. Bill was in the process of completing a correspondence course prior to joining the R.N.Z.A.F. and was awaiting a knee operation following a failed medical. Tom, on the other hand, was called up almost immediately.

After completing his assignments and spending nearly four weeks in hospital, Bill was awaiting the call from the air force when the New Zealand government beat them to it. It had reluctantly re-introduced conscription for army service in May 1940, although entry to the navy and the air force remained voluntary. Bill was called up and posted to Claudlands, a suburb of Hamilton, where he joined the 22nd Battalion of the Waikato Regiment and where, much to his chagrin, he was billeted in a cattle shed. He was kitted out and started six weeks of basic training that consisted mainly of 'square bashing', pretty much what he had been used to in the cadets.

He was then posted to Great Barrier Island where, apart from a scare when it was reported that the Japanese were about to land, there was not a great deal of action - although later in the war the regiment was to see more than its fair share as the Allies fought their way through Italy. Bill was on the island for eight months, carrying out shipping reconnaissance and driving light armoured vehicles ('Bren carriers'), before finally joining the air force at the end of **May 1942**, despite his knee operation having been unsuccessful.

He spent six weeks at the air base at Rukuhia, which was unfinished and didn't officially open as an R.N.Z.A.F. station until later that year, and he described his time there as *'looking busy but not being busy.'* On the **11th July 1942** he was posted to R.N.Z.A.F. Tauranga, the home of the Central Flying School, where, frustratingly for Bill, he served in the Air Defence Unit manning Bren guns on anti-aircraft mounts, still with no opportunity to fly. Bill said that at the time there was a feeling that the Japanese could attack at any moment and, despite having few opportunities to practise firing the gun, they took their responsibilities seriously.

A break in the monotony occurred at dusk one evening. Just as Bill and his comrades were preparing to stand down there was a burst of Bren gun fire across the paddock.

There was a big flap and the perpetrator was called up and he said that he was practising sighting the Bren gun and inadvertently the safety catch was released and the Bren fired. So that was the accepted explanation but when talking to him afterwards he said he saw a rabbit so he had a 'quiet' shot.

There was speculation afterwards about what a few rounds from a Bren gun would have done to the poor rabbit had he been a better shot.

Tensions in New Zealand had been rising with each fresh incident that brought the war closer. The sinking of the Niagara had been followed by the attack on the U.S. Navy at Pearl Harbour in December 1941 and the bombing of the Australian naval base in Darwin in February 1942. That signalled the beginning of a campaign of aerial bombardment on Australia that continued throughout 1942 and 1943. Like Bob, who had by this time been rejected by the R.A.F., Bill was desperate to play his part but still he had not been able to follow in his brothers' footsteps and start training as a pilot.

The problem for Bill, and others in his situation in **May 1942**, was that a large surplus of trained aircrew had built up in the U.K. and measures had been taken to extend the training period, particularly for pilots. Whether or not it was an intended consequence is unclear, but this extension improved the quality of flying and the rate of training casualties was halved between 1940/41 and the end of the war, from one in every 11,156 flying hours to one in 22,388.

Finally, on the **4th February 1943**, nearly two years after being conscripted into the army, he was posted to the I.T.W. at R.N.Z.A.F. Rotorua where he was billeted in the Brent's Hotel and, at the end of two months training and assessment, a short interview with the selection board confirmed Bill's recommendation for pilot training. Then, on the **4th April**

A DH82 Tiger Moth (picture: Tony Hisgett, https://creativecommons.org/licenses/by/4.0/)

1943, the day after Bob's 24th birthday, Bill was posted to No. 1 Elementary Flying Training School (E.F.T.S.) at R.N.Z.A.F. Taieri, about twenty miles from Dunedin. Two days later, Bill took to the air for the first time, in a yellow Tiger Moth DH82 piloted by a Pilot Officer Wilson., whom Bill described as *'one of the nicest guys I've ever met'*.

After watching aircraft for so many years, it must have been difficult to put into words the feeling of exhilaration that Bill felt taking that first flight. Sixty years later he made an effort during the interview with Martin Halliday, apparently unable to avoid the art of understatement:

Well, it was quite an experience. I'd never flown before – my experience was quite exciting. I had a very good instructor and it was a very enjoyable flight.

On the **12th April**, three days after his 23rd birthday and after about ten hours of dual flying, he took the controls and flew solo for the first time. He recalled that with a little more enthusiasm:

> ......*it was an exhilarating experience really, you know how you are in an open aircraft with the air rushing around you, the thrill of wearing your helmet and goggles – it was all something new and exciting really.*

On the **29th May 1943**, after just over six weeks training and sixty hours flying, twenty four of them solo, Bill was given a week's pre-embarkation leave before boarding the U.S.S. Matsonia in Auckland on the **4th June** and setting off on a six thousand mile voyage across the Pacific to

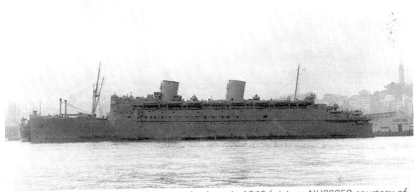

The U.S.S. Matsonia in San Francisco harbour in 1943 (picture NH89859 courtesy of the Naval History & Heritage Command)

the United States. It was carrying hundreds of aspiring pilots, navigators, bomb aimers and wireless operators en route to Canada, just as Bill's surviving brother Tom was sailing from Canada to England, having already been awarded his 'wings'.

The Matsonia, a liner requisitioned by the U.S. Navy and refitted as a troop carrier, docked in San Francisco two weeks later. It was only eighteen months after the Japanese attack on Pearl Harbour and there was an understandable nervousness amongst the U.S. military, although Bill was disappointed to be treated like the enemy. When asked in his interview if the Americans were friendly he replied

> *No, well when I say friendly, I mean the individual was friendly but they*

had a paranoia, would be best to explain it. They posted the guard on the ship and all that sort of business. They finger printed us. Nobody went ashore … I got ashore on the baggage truck and that was one of my own intuition or initiative and that was all I saw of San Francisco and then the rest of the blokes never saw even that.

They had arrived in the morning and in the afternoon were taken on a short ferry trip over to Oakland, where they boarded a train for a two day journey to Vancouver. There they made a quick transfer from the American Railroad to the Canadian National Railways and continued their journey with a three day trip to Edmonton.

There, at No.3 Manning Depot, they had a few days respite before continuing their trans-continental journey with a four day train journey to Ontario. On the **12th July 1943** Bill arrived at No. 5 Service Flying Training School (S.F.T.S.) in Brantford, Ontario where, in preparation for flying multi-engine aircraft, he spent the next sixteen weeks improving his flying skills in a twin-engine Mark II Avro Anson.

His first flight was on the day after his arrival and, as well as flying the aircraft, he was expected to carry out his own navigation and bombing practice under the tutelage of Pilot Officer McCartney, an Australian. Bill recalled that he *'got a fairly high mark'* on bombing and his log book seems to confirm that he was consistently graded as 'average' for flying and navigation but managed an 'above average' for bombing. It was whilst flying the Anson, a very different experience to flying a Tiger Moth, that Bill had to get used to flying with a parachute at all times.

Brantford aerodrome had been established in 1929 and had become a flying school for bomber pilots in 1940, administered by the Royal Canadian Air Force as part of the British Commonwealth Air Training Plan, also known as the Empire Air Training Scheme. It is only a hundred and seventy miles from Detroit and Bill managed at least one trip there to visit a New Zealand-born American and his wife, Nick and Olive. After the war they remained friends and Bill looked after them when they visited New Zealand.

Whilst at Brantford, just a few months after the 'Dam Busters' raids, the trainees were addressed by Guy Gibson on a morale-boosting

54

tour. When asked by Martin Halliday if at any stage he felt apprehensive about what might lie ahead for him Bill was unequivocal:

We were young, happy and the world was in front of us — you've got to treat it as an adventure.

Guy Gibson resumed operational flying the following year and was killed when his Mosquito crashed in the Netherlands returning from an operation.

Bill trained alongside Australians, Canadians and what he called 'R.A.F. types' in Brantford and in **November 1943** was presented with his wings by the Chief Flying Instructor, a Squadron Leader whose name Bill could not recall. He and a couple of friends then embarked on another epic train journey to Halifax, Nova Scotia. They travelled via Detroit, where he once again visited his friends, and New York, where they stayed in a cheap hotel run by the United Service Organisations and were given free tickets to a show.

In Halifax, they boarded the S.S. Mauretania, a Cunard White Star liner that had been requisitioned as a troop carrier just a few months after her maiden trans-Atlantic voyage in 1939. With the threat from U-boats in the Atlantic, there were daily lifeboat drills and it took about six days in cramped and cold conditions to ferry Bill and his fellow airmen, as well as thousands of U.S. and Canadian troops, to Liverpool. It was late November and D-Day was just over six months away. On the **2nd December 1943**, the men disembarked and Bill boarded a train for Brighton that had drawn up alongside their ship.

Even though Bill was now in the U.K. and expecting to see action fairly soon, he was to face further frustrations and it would be another fifteen months before he would be posted to an operational squadron. By the end of 1943 there were adequate reserves of aircrew, both fully trained and under training, and in February 1944 the Supervisory Board of the British Commonwealth Air Training Scheme decided that the output should be gradually reduced. By June 1944, a serious bottleneck had developed and a large backlog of pilots had accumulated in the U.K., New Zealand and Canada.

After a short train journey, at least compared to those in Canada,

Bill arrived at No. 12 Personnel Reception Centre in Brighton where he was billeted at the Grand Hotel, made famous in 1984 by the I.R.A. bomb attack on Prime Minister Margaret Thatcher and her government.

The photograph below, taken in March 1943, shows gunners of the Light Anti-aircraft Regiment, Royal Canadian Artillery, manning a 40 mm Bofors anti-aircraft gun near Brighton's West Pier, with the Grand Hotel in the background. They were guarding against 'tip-and-run' raids by German Focke-Wulf Fw-190 aircraft.

After relatively few internet queries, I was able to confirm that the

Brighton seafront, 1943 (picture: MIKAN 3223277, Library and Archives Canada)

young man standing behind the gun is twenty year old Gunner Bruno Anderson, whose daughter Peggy lives in Vancouver. Peggy told me that her father was a member of the Canadian Army Hockey Team and that he played many Army series playoff games whilst he was stationed in Sussex.

She also told me that the gunner at the lower controls was 'Mac', a friend of her dad, who was killed on Sunday the 23rd May that year when several Fw-190s dropped bombs on the town centre at lunch time.

'Mac' was probably Trooper Donald James McMartin, who was killed alongside ten of his comrades in the Albany Hotel, Hastings, used at the time to billet Canadian soldiers. The largest loss of life was in the Swan Hotel where as many as sixteen were killed. Bruno lost part of his leg in the raid and wasn't able to return to Canada until 1946 because of the extensive surgery required.

The memorial on the site of the Albany Hotel

Bill and his mates soon discovered how many pubs there were between the Grand and the railway station and their 'pub crawl challenge' was to make the journey whist having at least one drink in every one of them. They were there too late to bump into Bruno and his comrades.

We used to make our way gradually up towards the railway station and see if we could make it by the end of the night – one beer here or two beers there and move on.

Bill was in Brighton for about three weeks before being posted to R.A.F. Manston in Kent, fifty miles from R.A.F. Detling from where his brother Jack had flown to his death just three years earlier. There were no opportunities to fly at Manston but Bill enjoyed his time there carrying out 'flying control duties', later to be called 'air traffic control', for about six months. At least he was in the company of aircraft and it took him back to his youth watching Gypsy Moths with his brothers at Bell Block airfield.

There were Hawker Typhoons on permanent stand-by at Manston in 1944, with Tempests arriving while he was there, and it was an emergency landing field for disabled bombers. There was also a Fleet Air Arm section equipped with the Fairey Swordfish and the Supermarine Walrus for air sea rescue and Bill was in his element, though he longed to be in the cockpit. He was aware that it could have been a lot worse though – some pilots were posted to the New Zealand Army post office in London!

Manston was one of the few airfields at the time equipped with

F.I.D.O., the Fog Investigation and Dispersal Operation, designed to remove fog from airfields with burning petrol. Bill recalled many incidents of badly damaged aircraft landing on the emergency runway. He described incidents of bombs falling off aircraft and rolling across the runway and of aircraft crashing and having to have their bombs defused before they could be moved. It was clearly an eventful posting with some of the incidents having tragic consequences. *'We've seen many accidents there, some of them very tragic'* was how Bill remembered it.

Whilst at R.A.F. Manston, Bill became friendly with the senior officer in Flying Control, Squadron Leader Jock Leaper, who was a former WW1 pilot and, according to Bill, *'a delightful man to work with.'* S/L Leaper lived off station with his wife in the village of Manston and would cycle to work every day. Bill had a deal with him that if it was raining he would take one of the station's cars under the pretext of checking the outer lights, then collect 'Jock' and his bike. *'Security checks were never a problem with a Squadron Leader in the car'*.

Whenever he had leave, Bill would meet up with people he knew from home at the New Zealand Forces Club on Charing Cross Road in London, an 'all ranks' clubs generally considered to be very good for morale and described by Bill as a *'great set-up'*. During one leave he was able to meet up with his surviving brother, Tom – it was the last time he saw him.

Bill had by this time been in the military for nearly three years and Bob, who would join Bill's crew later in the year, had only just been summoned to R.A.F. Regent's Park, less than two miles away, to start five weeks basic training.

Bill was promoted to flight sergeant on the **29th March 1944** and remained at Manston until the 6th June 1944 (D-Day) when he travelled to R.A.F. Padgate, coincidentally where Bob had had his unsuccessful interview in 1942, on his way to an Advanced Flying Unit. Bill says he heard about the D-Day landings on the train to Padgate but he had been aware for some time that something was afoot, as it was impossible to miss the huge build-up of troops, tanks, vehicles and equipment near the south coast.

He arrived at No.3 A.F.U. in South Cerney, Gloucestershire on the

8th June 1944 and was billeted at R.A.F. Bibury, where there was a relief landing strip. Here, he was to become familiar with the Airspeed Oxford, another twin-engine aircraft used extensively in the training of Commonwealth aircrews, as well as navigation, map reading and night flying. It was the first time he had carried out night flying under complete blackout and for the first time he learned how to fly with reference to the instruments alone. He also had to get used to flying in what were described as 'English conditions' or, as Bill put it, *'bloody awful English weather'*.

By **August 1944**, Bill was ready to take on a crew of his own and, on the 22nd, he was posted to No.11 Operational Training Unit (O.T.U.) at R.A.F. Oakley in Buckinghamshire. There, he 'crewed up' with a navigator, a bomb aimer, a wireless operator and two gunners before being introduced to the Wellington bomber. They would have to wait another four months before Bob, who at this time was only half-way through his flight engineer training at St. Athan, would complete the Mallon crew.

5 THE MALLON CREW: 'ONE OF THE LUCKY ONES'

The Mallon crew minus Bob, who took the photograph, in December 1944. From left to right: Jim Haworth, Don Cook, Bill Mallon, Frank Symes, Denis Eynstone and Ken Philp.

Bill took the responsibility of selecting his crew extremely seriously, despite the rather haphazard method that was the accepted practice, as he was well aware that a mistake could have disastrous consequences for them all. Here's how Bill described the process of 'crewing up':

> *Well, we were thrown in a bunch, bunch of wireless operators over there, bunch of navigators over there and some gunners over there so you were told to try and make out self-compatible as you could to form your crew – fairly hit and miss in that sense. We didn't have time to actually evaluate an individual. You had to form your crew and that was to be it.*

First of all, he carefully scanned the navigators, standing in small groups and engaged in conversation towards the back of the Sergeants' Mess. The one he was drawn to had a rather serious look which Bill considered to be a desirable trait in someone with whom he would have to work closely and in whom he was to trust his life. It turned out, despite first impressions, that Jim Haworth, from the South Island of New Zealand, had an amazingly dry sense of humour and a real talent for writing.

Bill waited for a lull in the conversation and approached him. He introduced himself and asked Jim if he would be his navigator. He grinned, shook hands and the deal was done.

It turned out that Jim was the only member of the crew, until Bob joined them, who was married and the only one with children. It soon became clear that his serious demeanour was a result of having to leave behind his wife Sally, whom he had married in 1938, and his two little girls, Ruth, who was nearly five, and Maryann, who had only been a few weeks old when he

Jim Haworth

left New Zealand for Canada more than two years earlier.

Along with many of his countrymen, Jim had completed his training in Canada, under the British Commonwealth Air Training Plan, where he had started to write letters home almost daily, something he was to continue throughout his time abroad. It is Jim's letters that have provided so much of the detail for this story, as well as a valuable insight into the feelings of a young man with an uncertain future thousands of miles from home.

Born in Timaru in 1911, Jim was the oldest of the crew at thirty four and the only one with the benefit of a university education, having gained an Accounting Degree and the major part of an L.L.B studying part-time at Canterbury University, Christchurch. While studying he had worked for Timaru Motors, a branch of the Colonial Motor Company, which had the Ford Franchise at that time. He had set up his own practice as a Chartered Accountant after being admitted to the Accountants Society in 1933.

Bill had already decided that his bomb aimer should also be

someone with a bit of life experience and he and Jim cornered another Kiwi, Ken Philp, who, unlike so many of the fresh-faced young men waiting to be picked, didn't look as though he was straight out of training. Ken had already received a commission, becoming Flying Officer Philp in July 1944, and was approaching his thirty first birthday. Like Bill, he had a sister and two brothers but there was something else he had in common with his skipper - one of his brothers had trained as a pilot and had been shot down and killed in northern France.

Searching round the room for a wireless operator, the three men were drawn to a young man with thick, wavy dark hair and an engaging smile. Frank Symes was a mature twenty year-old from Wairoa, on the North Island. He was the fifth of eight children and his mother had died when Frank was only five. He had then been raised by his father, older siblings and later by his step mother, Lily, and, in 1941, when Frank was sixteen and working as a farm labourer on his Uncle Bert's farm in Waverley, Taranaki, his father Stuart also died.

Shortly afterwards, Frank decided to enlist and, in July 1942, he walked into the local R.N.Z.A.F. recruiting office and signed up. He was eighteen and later confided in his new

Frank Symes in Canada, 1943

comrades that he had only decided to enlist because the air force offered more excitement than labouring on his Uncle Bert's farm.

He was educated at Nuhaka Primary School and Hastings Boys' High School and, as well as playing cricket and football, he had been a member of the Hasting Boys' 1st XV Rugby Team. He had left New

Zealand for Canada in April 1943, where he trained as a wireless operator and air gunner and was promoted to Flight Sergeant.

All that remained was for Bill and his comrades to persuade two of the dozen or so young gunners milling around the mess to join them. Some, they agreed, looked barely old enough to have left school and it was two in this category on whom they eventually settled. Denis Eynstone, their rear gunner, was nineteen and became the youngest member of the crew and Don Cook, the mid-upper gunner, was a few months older having just turned twenty.

Denis Eynstone

Denis had harboured dreams of becoming a pilot ever since the Battle of Britain in the summer of 1940 when, as a fifteen year old, he had sat in a field in Oxfordshire attempting to identify the aircraft engaged in deadly combat above him. He joined the Air Training Corps and two years later, at the age of seventeen and whilst working as a clerk, he enlisted in the R.A.F.V.R.

He was *'recommended for training as pilot, navigator or bomb aimer (P.N.B.)'* but after over a year of training any hopes of becoming a pilot were dashed, as he was posted in May 1944 to No. 2 Air Gunnery School (A.G.S.) at R.A.F. Dalcross in Inverness. There was a shortage of air gunners at this stage of the war and a surplus of trained pilots and Denis seems to have volunteered for the role of gunner, possibly as a guarantee of at least getting in some operational flying before the war ended. After three months of gunnery training Denis was posted to Oakley to be snapped up by Bill as his rear gunner. Sadly, Don Cook remains a mystery, although his training will have followed a similar route to that of Denis.

Having assembled his crew, Bill had a relatively short time to mould them into an effective team before they started operational flying and I would imagine that their relationship was very much a professional one, particularly for Bob who joined the crew after the others had already been together for four months. How much they learnt about each other during this time is difficult to gauge but the fact that none of them, as far as we know, kept in touch after the war suggests they had insufficient time to become close, despite the extreme conditions in which they co-existed.

Before flying a Wellington for the first time at R.A.F. Oakley, Bill had to satisfy the 'Officer in charge of airmanship', Flight Lieutenant H. Hyde, that he had

... read and thoroughly understood the handling notes, that he fully

The entry in Bill's log book

understood the oil, ignition and petrol systems and the correct operation of the fuel cocks, including the nacelles, and that he was fully conversant with the oxygen system as fitted in the Wellington and with the use of the portable oxygen bottles.

These tasks were the responsibility of the flight engineer in a Lancaster bomber but they didn't yet have one and in a Wellington the pilot had to do it all.

The crew flew together for the first time on the **7th September 1944** and they had just eight weeks to blend their unpractised skills into an effective unit. As Bill explained, many years later, the crew had done very little flying and they all had to learn how to apply their expertise in a whole new context.

The wireless operator had to learn how to contact stations and ground control, the gunners had to practise air to air firing and air to drogue firing, and the bomb aimer bombing on bombing ranges.

In fact, the whole crew would have to develop an understanding with Bill that would improve their chances of hitting the target and getting home safely. Probably the most important of all in this respect was the navigator, Jim Haworth, with arguably the most technically challenging of all the roles and Jim would carry out this role impeccably.

On the day after the crew's first flight together he wrote:

Had our first trip last night but only as second navigator, which means you are only in the way. I was only going to wear an outer suit but when we got the met report I dashed back for the inner too, as when on a trip as second nav you have to work back in the body of the fuselage where it is open and no heating and plenty of drafts (sic). Supposed to climb up to fifteen thousand feet but had to climb up to twenty to get over some rough stuff. Believe me it was as cold as charity, about thirty below or more. I pitied the gunner in the tail. My mike soon froze up so I was cut off from the rest for quite a bit of the trip. The first nav's compartment is well heated, in fact too well heated, and does not need to wear any flying suit and even then complains of the heat!

Jim clearly followed the news very closely and was beginning to think that the war in Europe would be over by the time the crew was ready for operational flying:

Things are continuing to move pretty fast and if everything goes as at present, seems to me we will be seeing the east instead.

In other words, he was expecting to become involved in the war against Japan rather than Germany.

Whilst on exercises out of Oakley, there were a few incidents of German night fighters in the vicinity and in his interview in 2004 Bill recalled

We had a few scares there at night and ...we had to scamper off towards Wales or somewhere like that ... if there was a report there were intruders about to get the hell out of the road.

Another relief from the relentless training exercises was the day the crew spent assessing their physiological responses to flying at altitude using a decompression chamber. Bill's log book shows that, on the **2nd September 1944**, he was taken to the equivalent of 28,000 feet, much higher than he would be expected to fly with a full bomb load. He was deprived of oxygen by having his oxygen mask removed so that he could experience the symptoms in a controlled environment.

The crew clocked up seventy six hours in Wellingtons, with their

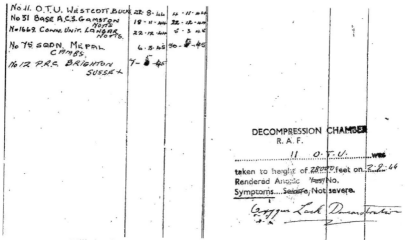

Bill's log book showing a record of the decompression exercise

last exercise taking place on the **2nd November 1944**. This was a two and a half hour night flying 'stick bomb' exercise, half of which involved flying on instruments. Records show that only about half of their flying time during this period was at night but Bill's recollection all those years later was that the *'biggest percentage would be night. Probably more night than day'*. With the stress involved in night flying, I can understand why it probably felt like that.

Once finished with the Wellington, they were almost ready to take on the extra challenge of the four-engine Avro Lancaster. They were given two weeks leave and then posted to No. 3 Aircrew School (A.C.S.) at R.A.F. Gamston, in Nottinghamshire, where they spent about a month waiting for a 'space' at one of the heavy bomber conversion units (H.C.U.s). This became available at No. 1669 H.C.U. at R.A.F. Langar, just nine miles from Gamston, and on the **22nd December 1944** the crew arrived for the final stage of their preparation.

When several new crews arrived at Langar, the day after his third flight with S/L Chipling, Bob eyed them with some suspicion. His survival would depend on him joining a crew who would be able to operate as effectively and as safely as possible. The last thing Bob wanted was to be a dead hero. He was approached by a young pilot with a strong New Zealand accent, who introduced himself as Bill Mallon and asked if he would join his crew. Bob agreed, they shook hands and Bill introduced him to the rest of the crew, three more Kiwis and the two young Englishmen who looked to be barely out of their teens. The Mallon crew was complete. Despite the arbitrary method of selecting his crew Bill later said *'I was one of the lucky ones - I managed to form a very compatible crew.'*

Jim wrote to Sally on the **28th December**:

Did I mention we have a flight engineer now, so have completed our crew? He is a married chap, the only other one in our lot. Think he's about twenty five and comes from Grimsby up on the Humber and seems quite a good chap.

I'm quite convinced this war is a single chap's one. Perhaps the Pommie ones who are married are not so badly off as they do get home leave. If I had known what I know now I would have plonked for N.Z. training and the Pacific. They do get back now and then. Think I will have to dry up and sign off before I show how bolshie I'm getting these days.

The extremely cold weather in Nottinghamshire, the coldest for fifty years according to the newspapers, reminded a home-sick navigator of where he and his wife had been living when he started his air force training.

I'm writing this hunched up over the stove in the hut. A good hard frost outside. We had a white Xmas here after all but not the sort of white one Canada might have had. It has been really cold over the last week with fogs up to the last two days, so that the country was white with hoar frost. I have never seen it so thick before, not even in 'Cargill. (Invercargill, on the southern tip of New Zealand's South Island) *'I've got my good old NZ army undergear on for the first time and feel like putting on long flying underpants to keep warm.. We only hope it doesn't get any colder as it must be about fifty below up top these days. Thank goodness the Lancs are well heated in the cabin. I'll need it.*

The complete crew of seven flew together in a Lancaster for the first time on the **28th January 1945**, with an experienced pilot, Flying Officer McGregor, and, after just a couple of hours dual flying, Bill was able to take over and fly solo. He found the transfer to four-engine flying quite straightforward and was thankful for the addition of a flight engineer.

The instrumentation is very similar, but a hell of a lot more, your main flying instruments were identical and so it didn't take long to be familiarised with it and happy to fly. It was a good aircraft to fly, especially with the extra pair of hands alongside me.

The training schedule involved circuits and landings, bombing practice, fighter affiliation and long periods of cross country flying to hone the skills of the navigator. Bob and his comrades would enter each step of their training in their log book as a series of numbered exercises and, whenever Bob climbed into the aircraft, he would have with him his emergency repair tool bag. Before, during and after every flight he would have to complete his four page Flight Engineer Log.

According to Jim, one 'fighter affiliation exercise' caused a great deal of hilarity amongst the crew. In a letter to his wife dated the **17th February 1945** he described what happened.

Bill chucked the kite around. Too much for my stomach, so when it came to the bombing exercise at the end I was 'fit for nowt'. Johnny, our rear gunner, was quite amused when I had to give a course for home while seated on the Elsan, the chemical lavatory aft in the fuselage. The engineer was just as bad as me, so I wasn't the only one.

I don't remember my dad ever mentioning that!

The crew had a total of about fifty hours flying time in a Lancaster in the month from the **28th January** to the **28th February 1945**, thirty six hours in daylight and twenty three hours at night. Sixteen hours of night flying were crammed into the last two days of February and Jim's letters to

Sally around this time reveal the rapid progress the crew were making. On the **7th February** he wrote:

> *Bill soloed today after 4 attempts to do the exercise so we will be pressing on regardless to finish the course'.*

And on the **17ᵗʰ February:**

> *We have now finished our day exercises and have only the night ones to do before being posted to a squadron which we understand will be at the end of this month – Bill has put in for a N.Z. one.*

Jim's description of the crew's penultimate night exercise, a mammoth six and a half hour flight over Britain, provides yet more evidence of his homesickness:

> *...we had covered a distance only about a hundred miles short of the smallest distance across the Tasman. If someone had told me a few years ago that I would be doing that distance at night I wouldn't have believed it.*

Once the crew had completed their H.C.U. training, they were considered ready for operational duty. Bob was officially declared qualified as a flight engineer for the Lancaster Marks I and III with effect from **1st March 1945** and the crew were granted three days leave. They were led to believe there would be six more once they received their next posting but they were to be disappointed. Bill and the other Kiwis were keen to be posted to a New Zealand Squadron and were delighted when they learnt they were going to join No. 75 (New Zealand) Squadron at R.A.F. Mepal, although none of them had any idea where Mepal

Bob's log book showing his qualification as a Lancaster flight engineer was.

The squadron, part of No. 3 Group Bomber Command, had become the first Commonwealth squadron in Bomber Command in 1940 when the N.Z. government made the airmen and aircraft of 'The New Zealand Squadron' available to the R.A.F. It was one of the larger, three-flight squadrons which, between 1943 and 1944, had about thirty five crews. By 1945 the squadron was practically 'double-manned', with two crews per aircraft, which would explain why the Mallon crew, assigned to 'B' Flight, flew in several different aircraft during their tour.

The squadron's motto was *'Ake ake kia kaha'*, a Maori phrase meaning *for ever and ever be strong'*. It was composed mainly of New Zealand personnel, although most of its flight engineers and many of its gunners were British and there were also airmen from many other Commonwealth countries. Equipped with Wellingtons from 1939 to 1942 it took part in the early bombing offensive against enemy-occupied territories and in July 1941 one of its aircrew, Sergeant James Allen Ward, was awarded the Victoria Cross, the highest Commonwealth award for valour, when he risked his life by climbing out on to the wing of his Wellington bomber to extinguish a fire.

Towards the end of 1942, the squadron converted to Stirlings and took part in a number of crucial operations before its ultimate conversion to Lancasters in 1944 and its move to Mepal, in Cambridgeshire, via Mildenhall and Newmarket. It flew more sorties than any other Allied heavy bomber squadron, suffered the second most casualties and was awarded many decorations in addition to Sergeant Ward's V.C.

The Mallon crew were now ready to play their part and, on the **6th March 1945,** they were posted to R.A.F. Mepal. But, instead of the expected six days leave, Bill experienced the full horrors of flak and night fighters the following night and, two days later, took his crew on their first operation.

6 OPERATIONS BEGIN: 'NOT MUCH FUTURE IN THIS GAME'

A Lancaster crew after a particularly harrowing operation over Germany in 1943, the tension etched clearly on their faces[1]

When the Mallon crew joined No. 75(NZ) Squadron at Mepal, the end of the war in Europe was just nine weeks away. On the Eastern Front, the German army was launching its last major offensive, Operation Frühlingserwachen or 'Spring Awakening', in the Lake Balaton area of Hungary, as it desperately attempted to hold on to some of its last oil reserves. It lasted just ten days. In Poland, the Germans in the fortress town of Grudziądz were on the verge of surrendering to the Red Army after a lengthy siege.

On the Western Front, American and Canadian troops had reached the Rhine and the U.S. First Army was fighting in Cologne, and in northern

---

[1] *In the course of my research I have seen hundreds of photographs of aircrews but none captures the tension experienced during an operation as well as this one. The origin of the photograph and the identity of the men remain a mystery, despite extensive research..*

Italy the U.S. Fifth Army was approaching Bologna. Although the end of the war was in sight and the German defences were seriously weakened, there was to be no easy run-in for the Mallon crew. Bomber Command was determined to pursue its campaign relentlessly, supporting the Allied advance and hitting fuel and transport targets until the very end.

The crew arrived at R.A.F. Mepal shortly after lunch time on Tuesday the **6th March 1945**, along with **F/O Bob Milsom** and his crew who had also just completed their training at R.A.F. Langar. The Milsom crew's bomb aimer was **F/O Lance Waugh**, who later joined the Mallon crew when 'Tiger Force' was being assembled, and its wireless operator was **F/S Randal Springer**, whose son Keith contacted me in September 2013 after discovering my blog.

Most of the details of the Mallon crew's operations have been gleaned from the crew's log books and the squadron's O.R.B. Because members of the crew were so reluctant to talk about their experiences to their families, Jim's letters and Bill's interview, both quoted extensively in italics, have provided almost the only insight into what the crew were actually feeling at the time.

The presence of familiar faces from home and from his navigator training was clearly a comfort to Jim. On the day after his arrival at Mepal he wrote:

The old gang is re-gathering again. String Staples is here, Slim Sommerville arrived today and Ken Dalzell is due to arrive in a few days.

These were all navigators from New Zealand whom he had met during his training in Canada but he also went on to mention familiar faces from back home:

One of the brothers from Rogers' Cycle Shop in Timaru has just finished. He has a good memory for faces as he remembered me. Have also come across another chap who was at Christchurch Boys' High with me.'

At two o'clock in the afternoon, on the day after their arrival, Bill presented his crew to the squadron's Commanding Officer, **Wing Commander Cyril 'Mac' Baigent**. The crew soon realised there was to be no additional six days leave when Mac greeted the new arrivals and told Bill *'you are flying tonight.'* Just before 5.30 p.m., Bill was airborne.

Mac Baigent had already completed two tours, fifty five operations in total, when he was appointed Commanding Officer of the squadron, ten days before his twenty second birthday in January 1945. He was the youngest squadron commander in Bomber Command and had been awarded the D.S.O., D.F.C. with bar and the A.F.C. He died eight years after the war at the age of thirty, cancer succeeding where flak and night fighters had failed.

All new pilots flew their first operation with an experienced pilot, generally referred to as flying '2nd dicky', so that when they took their own crew on their first operation they would have some idea of what to expect. It was not unknown for new pilots to be killed on this operation. Bill was flying '2nd dicky' with pilot **F/L Sid 'Buzz' Spilman** on a raid that virtually destroyed the German town of **Dessau,** just six weeks before it was taken by American troops.

He made it back safely early the following morning, despite what the O.R.B. described as a *'short inconclusive encounter'* with a night fighter, and the loss of eighteen Lancasters from other squadrons. For the first time doubts began to creep into Bill's mind.

We struck flak on the way out and on the way to the target we got a fighter. We had a pretty rough time all the way and then we got search lights over the target – I didn't think there was much future in this game.

'Buzz' told Bill on their return, maybe to reassure him, *'it was the worst night they'd ever had'*, and Bill concurred: *'it was the roughest night I'd ever experienced too!*

According to the relevant 'Combat Report', the encounter occurred at 2102 on the way to the target at an altitude of 18,000 feet. The mid-upper gunner, F/S Vernon Clouston, spotted a German Fw-190 fighter approaching from the port quarter at a distance of about six hundred yards. He immediately opened fire and gave the order to corkscrew to port. The pilot responded and the aircraft dropped about a thousand feet during the attack, the Fw-190 passing vertically downwards on their starboard side, having suffered damage to its wing and fuselage.

In a letter to Sally that evening, probably penned while Bill was having his 'encounter' with the night fighter, Jim wrote

Bill our skipper is on a second dicky trip tonight so you can see that they do not waste any time here before starting you to work. The rest of us will probably have our first trip tomorrow night.

Because Bill didn't touch down until 0210 the following morning, the rest of the crew had another day of rest before **Friday 9th March**, when Bill took them on their first operation, a daylight raid on Datteln in the heavily defended industrial Ruhr Valley. It was the day of Denis' twentieth birthday and not the way he would have chosen to celebrate it.

As the crew approached the aircraft, Bob had to overcome severe stomach cramps and nausea that got worse as he boarded the plane. He later said that he would experience these symptoms, together with hyperventilation and an exaggerated heartbeat, before every operation and that they would ease only when he became preoccupied with his routine of pre-flight checks on fuel, hydraulics, electrics and oxygen.

Their target was the **Emscher-Lippe benzol plant** and the operation was part of the so-called 'Oil Campaign' to deprive the German war effort of fuel. They were flying Lancaster AA-L (HK562), one of several of the squadron's Lancasters fitted with a mid-under gun which was manned by an eighth crew member, F/O Charles Frederick Green D.F.C. They were in the air for nearly five and a half hours.

In the meantime we have started productive work. First trip today - a daylight one and a very quiet one - may they all be like that! Couldn't see the ground... as it was fully covered with cloud. Only a short way into Germany to deliver our cargo.

Reference to the future and the progress of the war were recurring themes in Jim's letters:

The news today is very good. My own opinion is that it will not be very long now. I hope so...if the war finishes quickly over here they have had me for the East as far as I am concerned.

Despite their apprehension, I am sure that some of the younger crew members would have been looking forward to their first taste of

74

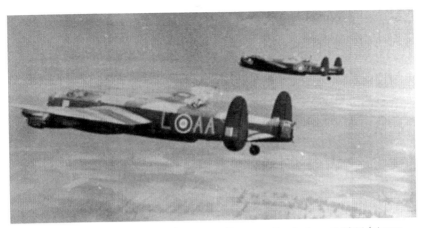

HK562 (AA-L), in the foreground, on an earlier operation in August 1944 (picture courtesy of Ron Mayhill)

action with a sense of excitement but not the eighth crew member, mid-under gunner Charles Green, who had long ceased to view his job as an adventure. Charles was only twenty three but had already taken part in over forty operations and was beginning to wonder when his luck would run out. He need not have worried – he was the only one of the crew still alive in 2016.

The following day, **Saturday 10th March**, saw the crew of eight on their second operation, a daylight raid on the **Scholven-Buer synthetic oil plant** in **Gelsenkirchen**. They flew in the same aircraft and again the flight was a relatively short one at just under five hours. Jim's description included a surprising amount of detail:

> *Yesterday's trip was about as quiet as the previous day's with some flak near the target but not amongst our lot. Another oil plant but not very far into the Ruhr past the front line, so hope ours landed on it, particularly the 'blockbuster'. Thick cloud so could not see anything.' 'Please don't worry over me', he added, 'I've a good steady skipper.*

The day after the Gelsenkirchen operation, Bob and the rest of the crew were posted to R.A.F. Feltwell, twenty miles to the east in Norfolk and a former home of their squadron. Here, they undertook training in the use of GH (or Gee-H), a radio navigation system that had been developed in late 1943. While they were away the squadron lost another crew when Flight Lieutenant **Eric Parsons'** aircraft was shot down attacking the **Heinrich Hutte oil plants** in the southern Ruhr town of **Hattingen.**

Bill arrived back at Mepal on the **17th March** to find a telegram with terrible news awaiting his return. Jim described what happened in his usual matter-of-fact way:

Bill had the bad luck of finding a telegram waiting when we got back with the news of his elder brother's death. He was flying Mossies and it is the second brother Bill has lost.'

The crew was then belatedly granted six days leave, during which Bob took them to his home town. Jim didn't go, preferring instead to visit friends in Kent, and whilst there he wrote:

The rest of the chaps have gone up to Grimsby to Bob's place to celebrate his first wedding anniversary. I'll bet they have sunk some beer today - not for me.

While the crew were on leave, the squadron lost three more crews. On the 21st March, whilst participating in an ill-fated raid on the railway and viaduct at **Munster,** aircraft AA-T, AA-R and JN-P were brought down, probably all by flak but AA-R may have been the victim of bombs dropped from above. The pilots were F/L **Jack Plummer** (R.N.Z.A.F.), P/O **Alfred Brown** (R.N.Z.A.F.) and F/O **Derek Barr** (R.A.F.V.R.) respectively.

After one more GH bombing exercise, the Mallon crew returned to operational flying on **Tuesday 27th March** with another daylight raid, this time on the **Sachsen benzol plant** near **Hamm**, also in the Ruhr Valley. For the third and final time they flew as a crew of eight in AA-L and the crew had their first near miss when their port inner engine was damaged by flak.

The crew's log book entries describe the incident in the simplest of terms. Bob wrote *'Port inner feathered. Hit by flak'* and Bill *'three engines – flak.'* Only later did the details emerge. They were carrying a bomb load of 11,000 lbs, nearly five tons, and Bill judged it to be *'very close to our last operation as we had copped a bit of flak on the run-in to the target.'*

The flak had passed through the oil cooler and caused it to lose pressure and, once Bill had instructed Bob to shut down the engine and feather the propeller blades, he completed the bomb run and they returned home safely. *'It's no trouble for a Lanc to fly on three engines'* Bill added.

Jim's next letter to Sally described the operation with a neat play on words and added a brief description of the near disaster at the end.

> *Another benzol plant in the Ruhr. We cooked some Hamm that day. And had the egg when we got back. We managed to collect some flak in the port inner engine, so came back on three, tailing well behind the rest of the squadron. Think we were about a quarter of an hour behind them so made quite good time considering.*

Their fourth operation, on **Thursday 29th March,** was yet another daylight raid, this time flying a different aircraft, AA-X (RF157) and without a mid-under gunner. As the Allies advanced further east and the Red Army further west, the squadron's targets were becoming more distant and this time it was the **Hermann Goering benzol plant** at **Hallendorf** in Salzgitter, central Germany. They were airborne for over six and a half hours and Jim gave a full description of the operation, not for the first time speculating on how much longer the war could go on.

> *On Thursday we were in a show which was the deepest penetration in daylight the RAF heavies have made so far, to a place near Brunswick. There was a whistle when the target went up but during the whole trip we did not have very much trouble with flak and none with fighters. Over the target was pretty dicey, in thin cloud and quite a bit of flak but nothing hit us. Full cloud over the target, thank goodness. These days with the 'special instruments' as the papers call them, everyone hopes it won't be clear over the target on daylights. Coming back we had some more stuff chucked up at us near the Ruhr but they should be out of business nearly by now.*

> *I think the English papers (as usual) were too damned optimistic and if you believed all they said it was all over bar the shouting. Quite a few here have been betting whether they will have to do any more trips. Myself, I think at the shortest, it will last another six weeks. I'm keeping my fingers crossed.*

Jim's prediction was pretty good - it was just under seven weeks to

V.E. Day. In the same letter, Jim informed Sally that the squadron had been visited by a V.I.P. from New Zealand, almost certainly a morale boosting trip but probably with one eye on the general election the following year.

This morning we had a visit from Sid Holland who is over here - only took him four days by air to get here from NZ.

Sidney Holland had become Member of Parliament for Christchurch North in 1935 and leader of the National Party in 1940. He was Deputy Chairman of the War Cabinet for three months during 1942 and Leader of the Opposition for nearly ten years until the National Party won the 1949 general election. The visit is not mentioned in the squadron's O.R.B.

On **Wednesday 4th April**, the day after his twenty sixth birthday, Bob was summoned by the senior officer of 'B' Flight, **S/L Jack Parker**, and given an order he had been dreading. The flight engineer of another crew was ill and Bob would have to take his place. This would be Bob's fifth operation and it was just as well that he was unaware that the risk of being shot down during your first five operations was later estimated to be about ten times greater than in later operations.

That night he climbed aboard Lancaster AA-M (ME751) and positioned himself alongside a pilot he barely knew with a crew even more unfamiliar. The operation would take them further into enemy territory than ever before and they would be in the air for nearly eight and a half hours. Their target was the **Leuna synthetic oil plant and chemical works** near **Merseburg** in eastern Germany, known as the 'most heavily defended industrial target in Europe.'

As they taxied into position, Bob was surprised to see that the aircraft taxiing ahead of them was JN-D, a 'C' Flight aircraft piloted by F/S John Wood. His flight engineer, a Scot Bob knew only as Dougie, had missed the final briefing because of oil pressure problems and Bob had expected them to abort the operation. He gave it no more thought as he carried out his own pre-flight checks and JN-D lifted off a couple of minutes before them.

Bob's pilot on this operation was **F/L Ian Taylor (R.A.F.V.R.)**, whose crew included three Australians, a Canadian and a

British gunner. Bob was more relieved than normal to return safely, although his relief was short-lived when he heard that JN-D had been involved in an unfortunate incident and had returned without Dougie, their flight engineer. He avoided asking for details of what had happened.

The following day Jim wrote:

Our Engineer Bob was sent on one on Wednesday night to take a chap's place, so he is up one on us now. If the bomb line goes much further in, we will be going to Berlin in daylight shortly, as the Yanks have done before. Don't worry over me, we'll get through.

Although operational flying was an incredibly intense experience, there would have been some time for socialising and the locals became very familiar with the antics of aircrew letting off steam in The Three Pickerels and The Anchor, pubs in Mepal and Sutton respectively. Everyone nowadays is familiar with the Haka and will have seen it on television but in 1945 very few people in Britain were even aware of its existence. During one of Bob's forays to The Three Pickerels he was privileged to witness it first-hand, performed by Maori members of the squadron.

On **Monday 9th April**, Bob was back with his comrades in the Mallon crew for a night raid on the naval port of **Kiel**. The German heavy cruiser 'Admiral Scheer' was sunk, or at least capsized in shallow water, and the 'Admiral Hipper' and 'Emden' were damaged beyond repair. The Deutsche Werke U-boat yard was also badly damaged by the force of nearly six hundred Lancasters. Three were lost, none of them from No. 75 Squadron, although bomb aimer Ken Philp twisted his ankle and had to spend a short time in the station hospital.

We got another trip last night, this time to the docks at Kiel - our first night trip so I had to work like a one-armed paper hanger. A case of P.Y.F.O. all the way in and back. Too much sea for Bill's liking. Quite a bit of flak going in and coming out but less in the target area than we expected. Even so, Frankie the wireless op and I both had our 'shutes' on while we made our run, just in case.

The Admiral Scheer, capsized in Kiel docks after the raid of 9th April 1945 (picture CL2772 courtesy of I.W.M.)

I'm still patting myself on the back today as I got us on the target bang on the required time and when I mean 'bang on' I mean not to the nearest minute but nearest six seconds. Not bad after doing about four hundred and fifty miles there. Between you and me, I think it was more by 'Guess and by God' than good management but Bill had to belt old 'Liefy' (their new aircraft) *along to do it.*

Ken, our bomb aimer, had the bad luck to twist his ankle last night and is now having a rest in the station hospital, so we may not be on again for a few days.

This was wishful thinking on Jim's part. On **Saturday 14th April**, the crew left Ken behind and took part in the longest operation of their tour so far, an eight and a half hour trip to **Potsdam**, fifteen miles south west of Berlin. Ken's replacement was **F/S Owen Willetts**, who had completed twenty one operations with the squadron in 1944 but had just returned to Mepal from a posting with No. 291 Squadron in east Yorkshire.

Their targets were the marshalling yards and military barracks at Potsdam and this was the first time since March 1944 that Bomber Command four-engine aircraft had entered the Berlin 'defence zone'. It was also the last raid by a major Bomber Command force on a German city, just three weeks before V.E. Day. No. 75(NZ) Squadron lost one of its airmen when the flight engineer on AA-T, **Sgt Allan Sliman**, a former professional footballer, was fatally wounded by a cannon shell when his aircraft was attacked by two JU88s at about 9,000 feet on the return flight. It was his first operation.

Allan Sliman during his football career (picture: Chelmsford War Memorial website)

We have done one more trip, on Saturday night. A really long one, in fact the longest we could do at present. Just fifteen miles from the centre of Berlin to a place called Potsdam, practically a suburb of the big city. We were lucky to get away at all as 'Liefy' was having some work done on her and we took off ten minutes after the others had set course. Still we soon caught the stream up before very long. It was quite daylight for a long way in and finally went in to the target with the previous lot – six minutes early. So my nav. was not so hot in timing. Still I think most were early. Plenty of searchlights and flak but both missed us. Coming back I could easily have gone to sleep two hours before reaching base.

Once again, Jim uses familiar territory to illustrate the distance flown:

Altogether eight and a half hours up. We could have crossed the Tasman and gone back for a third of the way again in the time.

And Jim speculates once more about how much longer the war will last:

Unless things slow up over here I can't see us doing many more trips now. The papers are very optimistic again but I still give it a few more weeks, perhaps a month.

Another long daylight trip of over seven hours on **Friday 20th April** took them to the oil storage depot and docks in **Regensburg**, in Bavaria, S.E. Germany.

On Friday last, the 20th, we did another trip – a daylight one, our seventh all told. This was a long one, to a place called Regensburg in Southern Germany on the upper reaches of the Danube. I didn't have time to look out but Johnny our rear gunner says it definitely isn't blue but a dirty brown. Beautifully clear weather the whole way. On the way

All twenty of the Squadron's Lancasters on their way to bomb Regensburg on the 20th April 1945 (picture courtesy of Mary Morris)

had quite a good view of some of the broken bridges on the Rhine. Couldn't make out the front line but we saw quite a lot of fires so that is where it must have been. When we were near it we could see the Swiss Alps in the distance standing out quite distinctly.

Fraid though that after going all that way our load was nowhere near where it should have been. Not our fault though but I knew we were damn well overshooting before Ken pressed the tit. Can't tell you how I knew.

On **Sunday 22nd April**, Jim wrote about a huge raid on Bremen in which they were not involved:

'The boys were out again today, but not our turn this time. Even so our last three have all been long trips, so we seem to have missed the short ones. Just our luck......'

Just their luck indeed - the squadron lost yet another Flight Engineer when AA-T (NF935), piloted by **S/L J. Parker**, was struck by flak at 17,500 feet over Wilhemshaven on the return journey. The aircraft returned safely but **Sgt Roy Clark** of the R.A.F.V.R. lost his life.

Jim speculated once again about how much longer the Germans could hold out in the face of such unrelenting pressure.

Suppose you are following the news as closely as me these days. Tomorrow should read most of Berlin occupied. Why they continue to fight on beats me. But it can't be very long now.

Hitler killed himself eight days later.

Tuesday 24th April marked Bob's and the squadron's final war operation, a daylight raid on the marshalling yards at **Bad Oldesloe**, between Hamburg and Kiel in northern Germany. This was their first operation in a fairly new aircraft, AA-W (RF127), although it had been flown on several operations by **F/Lt Vernon Zinzan** (R.N.Z.A.F.), whose crew included Bob Sommerville, Simon's dad. Jim was quite excited about their 'new' aircraft, which was to take on special significance for the crew's families nearly seventy years later.

Did I mention we have a new kite, W for 'Willie'? Quite a newish job with all the latest bits and pieces in it.

From Jim's comments it was clear that the German defences had all but collapsed:

The trip was a daylight one to a place called Bad Oldesloe above Hamburg. The tamest trip so far – not a bit of flak anywhere except for an odd burst crossing the coast. We were deputy-leader of the squadron but that's all.

It was to be Bill's last flight and, although Bob never mentioned it to me, it very nearly ended badly once again. Here's Jim's account of what happened.

He left his last trip in a blaze of glory by nearly doing a ground hop on landing. A tyre burst just as we touched down and he could not correct it enough to keep it straight so it turned off the runway and finished up facing the way we had come. Quite exciting… the fire section jeep was there by the time we had stopped… or nearly so… followed by the fire wagon and two meat wagons. Horrible disappointment to all concerned there wasn't even a bleeding nose. Anyway Bill's namesake 'Willie' has to have a new undercart now.

After this final 'adventure', Bill said goodbye to his crew and was very quickly shipped off to Brighton on his way to console his devastated parents and sister back home in New Zealand. Sorry as they were to lose Bill, the crew was more than happy with his replacement, **Flying Officer Eric Butler**, who was an experienced pilot who had completed a tour with the squadron in 1941.

Our new skipper is the oldest (in time) skipper on the station. He has not done any ops since last November until one on Bremen a few days ago. We didn't do that one. He had been in hospital for a while. Comes from Wellington - Eric Butler by name, F/O by rank and seems to be a good type.

On the **1st May 1945**, a week before V. E. Day, Eric took the crew on a humanitarian operation to the Netherlands, part of 'Operation Manna'. This huge operation and its U.S. equivalent, 'Operation Chowhound', were organised to relieve the famine, known as the *Hongerwinter,* that had developed over the winter of 1944-45 in the German occupied areas of the Netherlands. A ceasefire had been arranged with the local German commander to facilitate the drops and more than three thousand Lancasters took part in late April and early May.

The crew was one of twenty one from the squadron detailed to drop their packs of supplies on Ypenburg airfield, near The Hague. I can remember Bob describing the sight of hundreds of people visible below their aircraft waving as they made their low-level flight, an experience also described in the squadron's O.R.B:

The population were very excited. There was a great deal of flag waving and 'thanks' messages were seen painted on the roof tops.

Many years after the war, Jim's daughter Ruth remembers him meeting a Dutch expat through their shared love of dogs, who worked out that he had probably received one of the food parcels dropped by the squadron. Both men became very emotional.

A Lancaster, possibly from 75(NZ) Squadron, dropping supplies on Ypenburg airfield on May 1st 1945 (picture from the Hans Onderwater collection)

So, after just eight weeks of operational flying, the Mallon crew's war was over and they could ponder their futures. For some there was the fear of continued conflict in the Far East, for Bob there was the prospect of a new family and a brighter future. But for all of them the return to civilian life would not be without its challenges.

7 DOUG WILLIAMSON: 'CLOSE ALL DOORS AND EXITS!'

Doug and his sisters Pat (W.R.N.S.), on the left, and Audrey (F.A.N.Y.) in 1944

Despite Bob's war coming to an end, he couldn't stop thinking about what had happened to Dougie, the flight engineer on JN-D, during the Merseburg operation a month earlier. Everyone knew the aircraft had suffered damage from flak, as they had seen the evidence for themselves, but none of them quite understood what the crew meant when they said that Dougie had 'fallen out of the aircraft'. There was lots of speculation but no-one seemed to know the full story.

From early conversations with my dad, I had a pretty good idea what 'flak' was, a word I later encountered in the world of work as a metaphor for excessive or abusive criticism, but as a child I had little understanding of its true horror. The word itself comes from the German 'Fliegerabwehrkanone', meaning aircraft defence gun, and most flak was generated by 88 mm anti-aircraft guns, also used as anti-tank weapons, which fired fifteen to twenty shells a minute with a ceiling of between twenty and twenty five thousand feet. The Lancaster Mk III had a ceiling of about twenty four thousand feet but usually operated considerably lower. 105 mm and 128 mm guns with a ceiling up to about thirty five thousand feet were also used.

When the shells from these guns exploded they brought down planes either by direct hits or by the blast and fragments of shrapnel. An exploding shell within thirty metres would usually bring down an aircraft but serious damage could be inflicted within two hundred metres and many airmen were killed by flak in aircraft that returned relatively undamaged. A fuselage made from the aluminium alloy 'Alclad'[2], less than three quarters of a millimetre thick, would have given no protection to the crew inside, the only armour plating protecting the crew being situated behind the pilot's seat and head. A direct hit on a full bomb load would have left very little of the aircraft or crew.

German searchlights were fitted with sound locators and the guns had increasingly sophisticated devices to improve their accuracy, including shells fitted with transmitters so they detonated when they were at a pre-

---

[2] *'Alclad', a composite stronger and more resistant to corrosion than earlier light-weight alloys, is formed from high-purity aluminium surface layers bonded to a high-strength alloy core made from heat-treated aluminium, copper, manganese and magnesium. It has the corrosion resistance of pure aluminium at the surface and the strength of the strong alloy underneath. The Alclad sheets covering most of the airframe of a Lancaster were 22 SWG (0.71 mm thick), although some were 16 SWG (1.63 mm).*

determined distance from an aircraft. One particularly lethal method was to fire 'box barrages', where up to forty guns would each fire fifteen to twenty shells a minute to explode in a sphere about fifty five metres in diameter at the height that radar or 'predictors' (primitive computers) indicated the bombers were flying.

Anti-aircraft guns brought down more aircraft than fighters did, particularly in 1944 and 1945 when the Luftwaffe was at its weakest, but it has been estimated that the Germans fired three thousand shells for every plane that was shot down. On the 27th March 1945, the Mallon crew had an encounter with flak when an engine was disabled as they approached their target. So too did Flying Officer John Wood and his crew a week later. Both aircraft returned safely but only the Mallon crew returned with all seven crew members.

When the Wood crew arrived at dispersal just after 1800 on the 4th April 1945, the ground crew showed them a large circular hole cut in the belly of their aircraft, JN-D (HK601). A 0.5 inch Browning machine gun had been installed as defence against night fighter attacks from below but the crew were puzzled as they had not been allocated a mid-under gunner to operate the gun.

They had completed thirty one operations since their arrival at Mepal on the 2nd December 1944 and had been rather put out after their thirtieth when the size of a tour was increased from thirty to thirty five. Much to their relief it was then reduced to thirty two and this was to be their last operation before becoming 'tour expired'.

Flight engineer Sergeant Doug Williamson, a Scot from just outside Edinburgh, sorted out the bundles of 'window'[3], inspected the new gun emplacement and carried out his pre-flight checks. He was concerned that the oil gauge for the starboard inner engine was indicating zero oil pressure and was just about to shut the engine down and prepare to abort the operation when a quick tap of the gauge saw it jump up to the correct pressure.

---

[3] *Bundles of aluminised paper strips dropped from the aircraft to 'confuse' enemy radar, also known as 'chaff'.*

Doug had missed the final briefing and was unaware of their target but he had never seen so much 'window' before and deduced that this would be a long trip. He was correct - their target was the Leuna synthetic oil plant and chemical works near Merseburg, less than twenty miles from Leipzig in eastern Germany, a round trip of about eight hours.

JN-D lifted off at 1832 with no further indication of oil pressure problems, just two minutes ahead of AA-M (ME751), piloted by F/Lt. Ian Taylor. Alongside Ian was my dad, concentrating on helping the unfamiliar pilot get the aircraft safely off the ground.

Despite a number of incidents during their previous thirty one operations, Doug was convinced that he had a charmed life and says that at no time had he been frightened. On the contrary, he found flying in a Lancaster exhilarating and as they approached the end of their tour he was beginning to feel *somewhat depressed that the crew would be split up and all the excitement would soon be over.* He could not have anticipated quite how all the excitement would end.

As they crossed the Netherlands coast, Doug continued his routine of filling in his log and recording fuel consumption and oil pressures. He settled down on the floor by the 'window' chute and began tossing out bundles at prescribed intervals. Boredom began to set in and he longed for the operation to be over so that he could, as he put it, *'wallow in the glory of being 'tour expired.'* He remembered too late what he believed to be an old Japanese saying that the most dangerous point in a battle was when you relaxed and removed your helmet.

Doug relaxed, took out a bar of chocolate and removed his oxygen mask. Bang! According to the squadron's O.R.B. Doug's aircraft

was hit by flak before reaching the target, the bomb aimer (F/S Hooper) was burnt about the face and the pilot's hands were slightly burnt, the flight engineer (Sgt Williamson) apparently fell through the M.U.G. turret. The flak pierced the de-icing tank causing fire which destroyed several leads including heating to the A.S.I. (Air speed indicator).

Doug was later able to give his version of events:

I stood up and noticed small flickers of flame, much like you see on a

Christmas pudding. I was surprised to feel warm blood running down my face, as I had not felt any blow. I pushed my oxygen mask back up to my face and started the routine we had been instructed to carry out in training. **'Oxygen to emergency! Close all doors and exits!'** *I was thinking what a silly thing it was to say with a great big hole for the under gun emplacement at the back of the kite, when suddenly there was a woof and a huge burst of flame completely filled the whole passage down from the front of the kite. It was like a massive blow torch.*

I turned my back to the flames and in doing so pulled out my intercom and so was unable to hear any order from the skipper. I grabbed the plug and turned to replace it, but could not see where it was due to a wall of flame. I … assumed the whole kite was burning. It looked as if we had little time to get out, but I assumed the order had been given with little time to act. The escape hatch was in the bomb aimer's compartment and blocked by flame. I turned, moved back towards the rear and shouted to the wireless operator (Gerry Newey, the uncle of Chris Newey who has been such a help with my research) *that we would have to use the under turret to get out, clambered over the main spar, and collapsed.*

I lay there in a sort of stupor, probably lack of oxygen, waiting for the rest of the crew, but none came. I assumed we were doomed and were plunging earthward. My thoughts were on my end and I was surprisingly calm and curious as to what it would be like to be dead. I told myself it wouldn't hurt it would just be a big bang and all would be over. I then wondered how mum and pop would feel when they got the war office telegram. Then I thought it was silly just lying there when all I needed to do was to pull myself out through that gaping hole.

I heaved myself along on my belly and slid out into a wonderful couch of cool air. I told myself to count ten as instructed. One, two …… ten, then pulled the ripcord. The next thing I remember was being suddenly awake and horrified at what I had done. There was no aircraft plunging to earth in flames. I felt as a sailor must feel, having fallen overboard and seeing his ship sailing off without him.

I was hanging in the air and all I could see was a great white canopy over me. It was complete darkness and utter silence except for the gentle rippling of the parachute canopy.'

Back in the aircraft, Jack Pauling had managed to extinguish the flames and Gerry Newey and Albert Cash, the mid-upper gunner, were trying to figure out what had happened. They could scarcely believe that Doug had just disappeared through the hole in the fuselage. The pilot, 'Timber' Wood, had decided to abort the mission and, as he jettisoned the bomb load, he instructed navigator Jack Pauling to set a course for home. They immediately started a quick post-mortem investigation into what had happened.

It became clear that a small piece of flak had pierced the large reservoir of de-icing fluid situated under the step down to the bomb aimer's compartment and a jet of burning ethylene glycol had set fire to the bomb aimer's parachute and clothing. Believing, like Doug, that they were going down, the bomb aimer, Noel Hooper, opened the escape hatch which in turn caused a powerful through draft creating a blowtorch effect that sprayed flame and de-icing fluid all over Doug. It was not blood on his face, as he realised later, but warm ethylene glycol.

Fortunately, Jack was able to beat out the flames with his hands and the remaining bundles of window – just as well, because his parachute harness had been completely burnt through, making his parachute as useless as Noel's – and he was able to navigate a course home using the burnt remains of his chart.

When they eventually landed in their blackened and charred Lancaster, they discovered another reason to be thankful. The pilot had not pressed down the bomb door lever hard enough when he jettisoned the bombs and it had sprung back up again. The bombs had crashed through the doors, luckily without any of them exploding. Jack subsequently received the D.F.M. and John the D.F.C., their citation published in a supplement to the London Gazette on the 5th June 1945:

Although some of the flying instruments had been put out of action and in spite of thick smoke which obscured his vision F/O Wood retained control. Meanwhile, F/S Pauling had gone to the assistance of the bomb aimer, whose clothing was on fire. He succeeded in extinguishing the flames on the clothing of his comrade and afterwards turned his attention to the burning part of the aircraft. Greatly encouraged by his pilot, whose example of coolness in these trying moments was inspiring, F/S Pauling worked strenuously and finally he succeeded in putting out the fire completely. Afterwards, F/O Wood flew the aircraft back to this country.

This officer and his gallant navigator displayed the highest qualities of determination and devotion to duty in the face of most harassing circumstances.

Relieved as they were to be home safely, Doug's fate was a cause for serious concern for his comrades, especially after all they had been through together. But in understatement typical of log book entries Gerry recorded the terrifying experience thus:

Duty	Remarks (Including results of bombing, gunnery, exercises, etc.)		Time Carried Forward:— 283·05 145·05	
			Flying Times	
			Day	Night
WOP	MERSEBURG	HIT & ON FIRE		
		LOST ENGINEER		7·30
PASSENGER	mission — BASE		·50	
		TOTAL TIME	283·55	152·35

Picture: Chris Newey

What happened next to Doug is recounted in *'The Nazi and the Luftgangster'*, a book written jointly by Doug and his friend Lutz Dille and published by Elgin Press, New Zealand (ISBN 978-0-473-22086-0) in 2012. Lutz, whom Doug met in Canada several years later, had been a member of the German armed forces during the war. He had been visiting his father in Leipzig three days before Doug bailed out just a few miles from their intended target.

Doug described how he spent several days in the German countryside trying to evade capture before he was eventually apprehended by a couple of farmers armed with hoes. He was handed over to the authorities in Eisleben, about 40 km from their target, and kept in the local jail. A few days later, amidst the chaos of war, he was handed over to the U.S. army at about the same time as Lutz was captured by the Americans. Within a couple of days he had been flown home to England, where he learnt to his relief that the rest of his crew had returned safely.

Seventy years later, Chris Newey informed me that Gerry and Jack met up with Doug in London after his return to England and, on the 30th May, the three of them had lunch together at the New Zealand Fernleaf

Club, one of the New Zealand Forces clubs, in Lowndes Square, London. There they talked about Doug's adventures, the rest of the crew's experiences in putting out the fire and how they managed to get their charred kite home. Doug was apparently a bit sheepish, feeling that he had abandoned his mates, but they reassured him that was not the case and they spent an enjoyable afternoon *'putting a few away...'*

Like Bob, Doug had completed his flight engineer training at St Athan in Wales but there the similarity ends. He was born in August 1925 at Seafield House in Roslin, near Edinburgh, in rather more affluent circumstances than all of the Mallon crew. The household employed two maids, Doug and his siblings had a governess and the children were able to play in a large garden with its own orchard

After kindergarten he attended the boys' school Craigend Park in Edinburgh and then became a boarder at Clayesmore School, shortly after it re-located from Winchester to Iwerne Manor in Dorset. It was an eight hour train and bus journey from Edinburgh but such is the state of public transport in Britain today that it would take longer than that now, over eighty years later! A contemporary of Doug's at Clayesmore was Tony Hart,

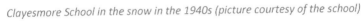

Clayesmore School in the snow in the 1940s (picture courtesy of the school)

93

the artist and television presenter, who was a couple of months younger than Doug and who died in 2009.

Doug was fourteen when war was declared, by which time he was attending Melville College, back in Edinburgh. He was evacuated to his Aunty Maggie's in Elgin, where he attended Elgin High school, his first experience of mixed sex education and large classes. Unfortunately, his Aunt was too old to cope with Doug and his two sisters so he returned to Melville College for another term before being evacuated again, this time to Argyllshire, where he attended Lochgilphead High School. Whilst there he joined the Home Guard, even though he was only sixteen and the official minimum age was seventeen.

He left school shortly after that in 1941 and continued his education with three months at Basil Paterson College. The following year, at the age of seventeen, he applied successfully to join the R.A.F.V.R. He was placed on reserve and spent two months at the Scottish Motor Transport plant before being called up for training, first of all at the A.C.R.C. at St. John's Wood and then at No. 20 I.T.W. at R.A.F. Bridlington.

After flight engineer training at St Athan, Doug was posted to No. 1657 H.C.U. at R.A.F. Stradishall in Suffolk, where he was to meet his crew, and they were then posted to No. 75(NZ) Squadron where they were allocated to 'C' Flight.

The full crew was:

- Pilot - F/S John Wood ('Timber') (R.N.Z.A.F.)
- Navigator – F/S John (Jack) Pauling (R.N.Z.A.F.)
- Flight engineer – Sgt Doug Williamson (R.A.F.V.R.)
- Bomb aimer – F/S Noel Hooper (R.A.F.V.R.)
- Wireless operator – F/S Gerald (Gerry) Newey (R.N.Z.A.F.)
- Mid-upper gunner - Sgt Albert Cash (R147847) (R.C.A.F.)
- Rear gunner - Sgt Ralph Sparrow ('Tweet') (R263518) (R.C.A.F.)

After the war, Doug had a short spell overseas with the R.A.F. before being demobbed and eventually moving to London to take up employment with Williams, a Dye Manufacturer in Hounslow, and continue playing rugby. In 1951 he accepted a three year contract managing a tea estate in India and shortly afterwards emigrated to Canada, arriving in Toronto in January 1955. It was here that he met his future wife Janet, also a Scottish immigrant, and they were married on the 31st May 1959.

It was in Toronto that he also met and became good friends with Lutz Dille, the co-author of '*The Nazi and the Luftgangster*'. Doug and Janet had two sons, Angus and Ian, and in 1968 Doug qualified as a member of The Professional Engineers of Ontario. He also tried his hand at teaching, not too successfully, and in 1972 the family decided to emigrate to New Zealand. On October 3rd, after saying their farewells to family and friends in Britain, they set sail on the 'Northern Star' from Southampton to Wellington.

It was in New Zealand that he finally found a job that gave him the satisfaction he had been seeking for so long, described in his book as '*the last and the best job I ever had.*' He became a tutor in the engineering department of The Technical Correspondence Institute, later to be re-named The Open Polytechnic of New Zealand. He retired at the age of 65 in 1990.

Moving to New Zealand also gave Doug the opportunity to renew old acquaintances. The three Kiwis in Doug's crew had all kept in touch after the war and Doug eventually met up again with his old pilot John Wood and navigator Jack Pauling. Sadly, wireless operator Gerry Newey had become yet another victim of cancer when he died in 1977, and Doug was unable to renew his friendship. Doug did meet Gerry's nephew Chris, though. Here's how Chris tells the story:

> *When I first heard about Doug's adventure … I had no idea that he was still alive and living here in Auckland. I had fired off a hopeful email and will never forget the phone ringing: 'Hi, this is Doug Williamson, I flew with your Uncle Gerry'! Turns out Doug used to live nearby and his two boys went to the same primary school as my two boys! A true gentleman, and one of the nicest people I have ever met, he and Janet have become good friends - Sandra and I were honoured to be invited to Doug's 90th birthday shindig earlier this year (2015). It is a special thing to be able to re-establish a connection that Doug and Gerry made 70 years ago.*

Doug, pictured in 2012 at Auckland's Museum of Transport and Technology (M.O.T.A.T.)
(picture: Doug and Janet Williamson)

In September 2012, thanks to an enormous act of generosity, Doug and four other R.A.F.V.R. veterans living in New Zealand were able to fly business class to London to see the R.A.F. Bomber Command Memorial statue in Green Park, unveiled by the Queen three months earlier. The trip, including a two week stay in the nearby R.A.F. Club, was funded by Ian Kuperus, founding director of T.M.N.Z., as a token of thanks for saving his father's life. Ian's father was one of thousands of Dutch civilians saved from starvation by 'Operation Manna' in which No. 75(NZ) Squadron had played such a large part.

8 THE WAR COMES TO AN END: 'IT PROBABLY AGED YOU …'

Children celebrating V.E. Day amongst the rubble of bombed homes in Battersea, south London (picture G3ARM6 courtesy of Alamy)

The war ended very differently for Bob and for Bill. For Bob, there was the gradual winding down of his service career, a return to a secure job in the fire service and the prospect of a settled family life. Vera was expecting their first child in the New Year and a Labour Government was elected in July 1945 with 48% of the vote and a huge majority. Bob was confident that their policies on welfare, education and public ownership would improve the lives of the British people and he couldn't have been more optimistic.

Bill, on the other hand, had lost both his brothers and, having survived the last few operations of the war, now faced a mammoth journey back home to his devastated parents and sister. In his letters to Sally, Jim described the slow progress in getting Bill a 'compassionate posting', something he had only agreed to on condition that he was transferred to New Zealand immediately.

18th March: *Bill Mallon was asked today if he wanted a* *compassionate posting back to NZ owing to the death of his second brother. After talking it over, he has cabled his people and is leaving the decision to them. Looks to me we may lose him, worse luck, as he is a good steady type. Still, my own opinion was that he should accept for his people's sake.*

31st March: *Bill is still waiting to hear from his people but from little bits I hear, it looks as if he will have no say in the matter.*

4th April: *Bill, our skipper, is still waiting a reply from his people in NZ, but just from what he has been saying I think he has made up his mind that he will apply to go back home. The way things are in Germany, the war may be practically finished before the H.Q. make up their mind, if he does want to go.*

10th April: *Bill is still waiting for news though I believe the matter is right out of his hands and to hear the Wing Co. has cabled NZ about him, we will probably lose him soon. If that happens we have no idea what they will do with us.*

13th April: *Bill has heard from his people, they want him to go back. So now he is waiting for NZ to OK the recommendation. His commission is due any day now so he will be OK for a good comfortable trip back home. He gets that as captain of a heavy bomber.*

25th April: *Bill has been told that he is being repatriated so the C.O. has pulled him off ops. He let him go on our last one yesterday, our eighth, before telling him. Bill will be just mucking about for a while until he goes down to the dispatch centre to catch a boat. He'll be like a lost sheep. We are sorry to lose Bill as we have been together nearly eight months now. I'll be giving him your address before he goes.*

So, immediately after their last operation, Bill packed his bags, said his goodbyes to his crew and waited to be discharged. It would be another nine weeks before he set foot on New Zealand soil again. He first returned to No. 12 Personnel Reception Centre in Brighton, the main New Zealand manning depot in England, where he had been posted eighteen months earlier, and waited there until a ship was available.

He didn't have long to wait, much to the consternation of those who had been waiting for several months, and was soon on a train back to Liverpool. On the 30th May 1945 he boarded the S.S. Arundel Castle, a Union Castle liner, and set off on a five week journey alongside several

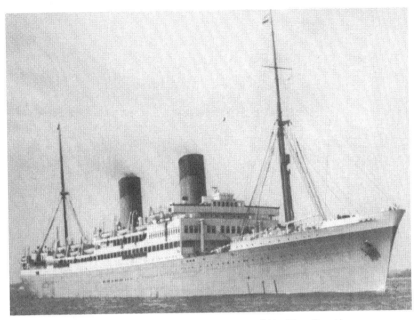

The Arundel Castle (picture courtesy of MaritimeQuest)

hundred Australian and New Zealand ex-P.o.W.s.

They passed through the port of Cristobal at the Western end of the Panama Canal on the 16th June and he was half way across the Pacific a week later when he was granted a commission in his absence, becoming the third Mallon brother to become a Pilot Officer. His commission was back dated to take effect from the 25th March.

The Arundel Castle docked in Wellington on the 3rd July, with Bill disappointed that they hadn't dropped off the Australians first at Sydney, because he said he would have liked to have had *'a look around Aussie'.* The ship set off for Sydney with the Australians two days later and spent nine days there. Bill was driven to New Plymouth in an army vehicle, having missed the train because of delays in receiving clearance, and was eventually discharged and returned to civilian life, his epic journey over.

Meanwhile, back in Cambridgeshire, bomb aimer Ken Philp had left to join No. 9 Squadron and Lance Waugh, whose crew had been posted to Mepal on the same day as the Mallon crew, took his place. The crew continued until the 6th July with cross country and army co-operation exercises, circuits and landings, fighter affiliation and bombing and air-sea firing practice in and around Britain. They even took part in a long range 'Bullseye' operation to southern France, an exercise designed to simulate a night time operation, and a 'Post-mortem' operation involving a flight over Germany to test captured radar equipment.

All this time, New Zealand officers and N.C.O.s were being transferred to R.A.F. Mepal from other squadrons as the squadron reverted to its original all New Zealand composition. They were still unsure whether they would be repatriated or shipped to the Far East for the next phase of the war.

Bob was one of a dwindling number of R.A.F.V.R. personnel still at Mepal and, just before the squadron moved out, he was granted leave until his next posting. On the 21st July, the whole squadron was transported to R.A.F. Spilsby, with No. 44 (Rhodesia) Squadron moving in the opposite direction.

After the war, the ministry was unsure what to do with the thousands of airmen and ground crew who were surplus to requirements and, in the summer of 1945, Bob had a temporary 'holding' posting at R.A.F. Burn in Yorkshire, formerly the home of No. 578 Squadron. It was there that he was put to work on a local farm and where he encountered yet another threat to his well-being, this time from a rather unusual source.

Many of his fellow reservists were city boys and, after months of hostility encounters over Germany, were as ill-prepared as Bob for this next challenge. Hector and Hercules were two huge boars, who not only terrorised the airmen but were also in competition for the affections of a particularly attractive sow. On one occasion, the sow had to be moved on a tractor-drawn trailer and one of the boars chased it all the way down the farm track, scattering Bob and his terrified comrades in all directions.

The scene was later described by my brother, with typical artistic licence, as being *'similar to the Land Rover being pursued by a T. Rex in Jurassic Park'*. The large pack of lard that Bob took home on his next leave produced a smile on the faces of his wife and mother, and more than made up for the fear he had felt facing five hundred pounds of rampaging boar.

His next move, on the 25th August 1945, signalled a change in direction for Bob, from aircrew to ground crew. He was posted to No.12 S. of T.T. at R.A.F. Melksham, in Wiltshire and re-mustered as 'Flight Engineer/FME under training'. In other words, he was to be trained as a Flight Mechanic (Engines). His flying days were over.

Meanwhile, with the war now over in the Far East, the decision was made to disband No. 75(NZ) Squadron and gradually, from October onwards, all of its personnel were shipped back to New Zealand. A new squadron was created in New Zealand the following year, No. 75 Squadron R.N.Z.A.F., which was controversially disbanded fifty five years later in 2001.

In November 1945, Bob was promoted to Flight Sergeant, exactly a year to the day after he qualified as a Flight Engineer and became a Sergeant, but it was not to last. On the 28th December, after four months of training, Bob once again passed his exams, this time a Local Trade Test Board (L.T.T.B.) assessment, and was re-mustered as a Flight Mechanic (Engines) and reverted to the rank of AC1 (Aircraftsman 1st Class), presumably because he had reverted to a ground trade.

His final posting, on the 11th January 1946, was to No. 1384 Heavy Transport Conversion Unit (H.T.C.U.) at R.A.F. Ossington, in Nottinghamshire, a unit under the control of R.A.F. Transport Command, where he worked on the Douglas Dakota, the Airspeed Oxford and the Avro York.

On the 19th January 1946, Bob's first child was born, Robert Jay junior, and two weeks later he was granted an emergency extended leave to go home and clear their new home of the bed bugs Vera had discovered in the bedrooms, with one alongside the baby in his cot. Two months later, on the 9th

Robert Jay junior, 1946

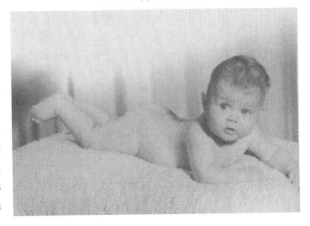

April, he was sent to No.100 Personnel Dispersal Centre in Uxbridge, West London, where he received his civilian ration book, his 'demob' suit and his outstanding pay. He was then 'released', although according to his service record his 'effective date of release' was 30th April, and placed on Class 'G' Reserve (R.A.F.), meaning he would *remain liable to recall to Air Force Service in an emergency'* during the next twelve years.

He re-joined the Grimsby Fire Brigade, where he stayed for just over two years. During my research, I came across a newspaper cutting from the Hull Daily Mail that told of an incident about which I knew only the flimsiest of details and which my dad brought up whenever my brother expressed an interest in owning a motor bike. It was dated the **29th September 1947** and showed that flak, German fighters and boars were not the only threat to Bob's life.

The headline 'TYRE BURST, TWO HURT' was followed by a short news item on what must have been a quiet day in Hull.

> **TYRE BURST, TWO HURT**
>
> The bursting of a motor cycle tyre in Beverley-rd., Hull, on Saturday evening, resulted in two men being treated for injuries at Hull Royal Infirmary.
>
> The injured men were Arnold Grimes (42), of 115, St. Philip's-rd., Sheffield, but in lodgings at 217, Cowper-rd., Grimsby, driver of the motor cycle, and Robert Jay, NFS fireman, of 15, Douglas-rd., Grimsby, pillion passenger. Grimes was detained at the Infirmary with head injuries, but Jay was allowed to go after treatment.

The bursting of a motor cycle tyre in Beverley Rd, Hull, on Saturday evening, resulted in two men being treated for injuries at Hull Royal Infirmary.

The injured men were Arnold Grimes (42), of 115, St. Philip's Rd, Sheffield, but in lodgings at 217, Cowper Road, Grimsby, driver of the motor cycle and Robert Jay, N.F.S. fireman of 15, Douglas Road, Grimsby, pillion passenger. Grimes was detained at the Infirmary with head injuries, but Jay was allowed to go after treatment.

Despite the errors in the addresses of the two men, it should have been Cooper Road and Douglas Avenue, this was my dad's story. I remember him telling us they were on a Brough Superior SS100, with a 998 c.c. engine, when they came off at sixty miles per hour but I had no idea that the accident had occurred in Hull. Apparently, he was wearing his flying leathers and boots at the time and, if it hadn't been for them, particularly the boots, he would have sustained much more serious injuries. His boots were so badly damaged that they had to be thrown away afterwards.

I was shocked to learn how close he came to losing his life in his flying gear whilst not actually flying, and by then he had two little boys at home, one of them, me, only two months old.

Bob, in 1937, showing an early interest in motor bikes – his accident ten years later brought that to an end

If he had died, he would have been in good company. T. E. Lawrence, 'Lawrence of Arabia', died when he crashed his Brough Superior SS100 in Dorset in 1935. A fully restored 1926 SS100, believed to be the bike that T. E. Lawrence used to race a Bristol fighter plane along the A15 in Lincolnshire, was sold at auction in London in 2012 for £280,000!

None of us is sure why Bob was in Hull, or who Arnold Grimes was, but the most likely explanation is that he was involved in work for the Fire Brigades Union (F.B.U.). The National Fire Service had been set up in August 1941, amalgamating the national Auxiliary Fire Service (A.F.S.) and the local authority fire brigades, and after the war the Fire Services Act of 1947 split the two organisations once again and returned responsibility for fire brigades to the local councils

Local politics, proposals for redundancies and the shabby treatment of returning servicemen led to serious disagreements between the F.B.U. and their employers. Disillusioned, and in solidarity with a number of his colleagues, Bob left the fire brigade shortly after the implementation of the Act and took on labouring work before joining the workforce of the new Fisons fertilizer factory that started production in 1951. He went on to work as a fitter in the chemical industry for the next twenty three years until his death in 1974.

Although Bob had been keen to take the fight to Nazi Germany, he eventually developed serious reservations about the 'Area Bombing' strategy introduced early in 1942. The purpose of Area Bombing had been laid out in a British Air Staff paper dated 23rd September 1941:

The ultimate aim of an attack on a town area is to break the morale of the population which occupies it. To ensure this, we must achieve two things: first, we must make the town physically uninhabitable and, secondly, we must make the people conscious of constant personal danger. The immediate aim, is therefore, twofold, namely, to produce (i) destruction and (ii) fear of death.

I suspect Bob would have taken some consolation from the fact that all of his operations involved military targets, although he was well aware of the devastating effect of any bombing on the civilian population and he wasn't the only one of the crew to harbour doubts about the campaign. Denis Eynstone was haunted for the rest of his life by thoughts of their victims on the ground.

When Bill was asked if the war had changed him, he didn't find it easy to answer:

I suppose it did — I suppose — well of course I was older — more experienced in the world in those sort of things I suppose it must have changed me — must have — it gave me a different outlook but I was still a young man, still a free man, single.

When asked what experiences in the war he was not going to forget, he was somewhat clearer:

I suppose it was operational flying probably, though I didn't do a long time, but I think it matured me, particularly to be placed in the situation of captain of an aircraft. You had an obligation to your crew, you certainly found that you had a responsibility that you had to undertake and live up to. I'm sure that responsibility was one of the most significant things that happened in your life. It probably aged you in that sense.

Did he have any concerns about killing people?

Not really, no, I knew that would happen but it was remote as far as that side of it goes. You were given a job, you were told to do it and told to do it to your best ability and you endeavoured to do that and you knew that if you didn't do it, that you'd be told about it.

Bill said he was proud to have had the opportunity to captain an aircraft and be in charge of a crew.

They depended on me and I depended on them.

Although it seems a waste that, after nearly three years of training, he was operational for less than two months, it is more of a waste that after his return to New Zealand he never had the opportunity to pilot an aircraft again. These missed opportunities, though, were nothing in comparison to those of his two brothers.

Bill, after receiving his medals in 1946

Bill married Lorna in 1950 and they had two sons, whom they named Barrie John and Kevin Thomas, thus keeping alive the memory of Bill's brothers. After sixty years of marriage, Bill died on the 29th June 2010 at the age of ninety.

Bob returned to a life packed with work, politics, union duties and family responsibilities. He and Vera had two more children after he was demobbed, Vic, who was born in 1947, and Pam, who was born in 1950 and given the middle name Phyllis after Bob's older sister. Phyllis had already begun to show worrying signs that she was ill when Bob returned after the war and, with understanding of mental illness at a pitiful level at that time, she continued to deteriorate.

High expectations, worry about the absence of her two brothers on war duty and alarm at the effects of the bombing of her home town, particularly the destruction of her beloved library, were all reasons the desperate family grasped to explain her condition. Fred and Sarah, supported by their two sons, struggled valiantly for several years to manage

Phyllis's condition, diagnosed at the time as schizophrenia, until the cruel intervention of a stroke in 1953 rendered Sarah no longer capable of caring for her. It was eventually reluctantly agreed that Phyllis should be admitted to St. John's Hospital in Lincoln.

Built in 1852, and originally called Lincolnshire County Pauper Lunatic Asylum, St John's was renowned at the time for its use of Electroconvulsive Therapy (E.C.T.), or 'electric shock treatment'. Just as we will never know the true cause or nature of Phyllis's condition, we will also never know the effect that years of incarceration, medication and E.C.T. had on her.

She was visited by her parents and/or her brothers every Sunday for over thirty years, before being transferred to a care home in her home town, just before St. John's eventual closure in 1989. Phyllis died in April 1990, outliving both her parents and her younger brother, Bob, who had died fifteen years earlier.

Bob suffered from stomach problems throughout his working life and blamed everything from shift work to exposure to chemicals at work. He even pointed out the similarity in symptoms to those he had suffered before every operation over Germany. His eventual diagnosis of stomach cancer came too late to prevent it spreading to his liver and he died at home late in the evening of the 3rd September 1974. He was fifty five.

9 JIM HAWORTH: 'HOME AT LAST'

Jim Haworth in about 1917

Jim remained with the crew throughout the summer of 1945, albeit a much changed crew. It had lost Bill for compassionate reasons and Ken had been transferred to another 'Tiger Force' squadron. Bob, Denis and Don had been re-assigned as the squadron became exclusively Kiwi and Jim was feeling very unsure about what the future had in store for him. He was desperate to go home and continued his letter writing until his ship finally docked in Wellington in November 1945.

What seems to have got Jim through the fear and frustration of over two years away from his young family was the ability to see the humour in any situation, no matter how dark, and then write about it in his letters to Sally. He was particularly amused by the workings of the air force and its attempts to keep the men happy, and a recurring theme in Jim's letters is food.

*When we go on these day trips or night trips too we seem to lose a meal. The egg (one) we get before and after is a poor makeweight. I really felt like the little pup being rewarded when we got back from our first trip. When we went in to the usual interrogations we were given a cup of tea **plus** one **chocolate** biscuit. I felt like wagging my tail and couldn't resist some sarcasm.*

By the way, I forgot to mention that after a night trip, we get a tot of rum before being interrogated. Makes me feel like a good little dog again.

After the squadron's war operations came to an end, Jim continued to write letters home every two or three days giving Sally, not to mention the readers of my blog seventy years later, some fascinating details of the squadron's activities during its final few weeks at Mepal, as well as Jim's views on the progress of the war.

May 4th 1945: ... *we were again on supply dropping near The Hague. Six hundred kites on that day. The day after we were up early to help load up for the next lot. We get a trip one day and a turn in loading the next. By tonight's news the boys are now on the job of bringing prisoners of war back from Germany. The idea is to pack in about twenty-six into a Lanc. What a scrum it will be.*

By the time we get back to camp from leave it looks as if the scrapping will be over altogether unless the Germans continue to hold out in Norway. Yesterday they gave in Italy... today in Holland and Denmark, tomorrow perhaps the rest of them. So I think I can say we have done our last op from England. What they do with us afterwards I can't guess. But the fact remains that even if we are sent back home it may be six months before there is transport. Even the repat. P.O.W.s may be held up over here for a while and they will have first preference. Still home for Christmas is what I am hoping for.

May 12th 1945: *The squadron is at present on the job of bringing back P.O.W.s from France. We are not on the order tomorrow either so have not had a turn yet. Lancs are flying back ten thousand a day at present.*

May 15th 1945: *Yesterday we went up with Eric and did a couple of circuits and landings, so we could do our turn at bringing back some P.O.W.s. We had not flown for about eleven days hence the need for C and L's. About half the crews here, including us, have been picked to the job of passenger carrying until the P.O.W.s are all back. The others are starting a training programme of training flights and whatnot.'*

There are all sorts of rumours of what is going to happen to us or where we are going but nothing official yet. It is rather early to hear something definite anyway.

May 17th 1945: *Incidentally, on the bus coming back from Cambridge I met a repatriated New Zealand P.O.W. He had been in Germany for three years and had arrived over here a few days ago. Turned out he was only six miles from the spot we pranged in our last op near Lubeck. So he was able to tell me what it was like on the ground that day.*

We were taken off the select list (carrying P.O.W.s) owing to the fact that Eric has done so little flying in the last six months through being in hospital. So we are on training trips instead. You may be wondering what all the training is for now things have finished over here.

Jim was still in the dark over what the future held:

Here's a knock my dear, it looks as if we have another job to finish off first in the Far East, so as I haven't done a tour over this side or been away more than two years, it appears that the chances of my coming back for some leave first are slim. I have learnt that there is an age limit of 35 for aircrew, so I'm going to enquire all about it. Anyway I still have a few months to go before I reach that. Still, keep your fingers crossed for me and it might come out the right way in the finish. As things are we have no idea who, when and how we will go, but it will probably take some time for bases to be completed out there. You may hear things over there earlier than we do, so keep the old waggers open and let me have any news you hear, particularly about chaps like me in the Army. I'd hate you to exist on Army pay though.

It was less than two weeks since V.E. Day, but after months of intense action boredom was beginning to set in:

May 20th 1945: *We are still sitting on our backsides, doing very little although there is a lot of bolony doing here, because of a visit in a few days by the C in C. So we have been filling in time doing various jobs, cleaning weeds and whatnot. Up to now we have only 5 hours flying this month.*

It's very boring when there is nothing to do except relaxing and doing nothing. I've been to the pictures three times and an Ensa show (the Entertainments National Service Association) *last night. That was simply pure unadulterated filth, nothing less, and not worth seeing. Tonight I saw 'the Prisoner of Zenda' on the station.* (a 1937 film based on the 1894 novel by Anthony Hope and starring Ronald Coleman, Madeleine Carroll and featuring Douglas Fairbanks Jr. and David Niven)

The immediate future was still uncertain for New Zealand and other Commonwealth air crews as the war continued unabated in the Far East.

From all we hear it appears that some of the crews here will be kept here as part of the Police Force. If it is a choice between that and the East you can guess which I would prefer, if there is no chance of returning in the meantime. Incidentally the Aussie in the lot moving out tells me he believes all Aussies will be going back before going elsewhere. Seems we Newzies are just the mugs. The Canucks (Canadians) *are doing the same as the Aussies.*

We are shifting over tomorrow with Shorty Baxter and co as the other lot who were with them are going on indefinite leave after nearly finishing a tour. We'll have more congenial company then.

This refers to F/S Rex Baxter, the navigator with the Milsom crew who had been posted to Mepal on the same day as the Mallon crew.

The training programme does not appear to be as strenuous as it was made out to be. I think the section leaders are just as browned off as we are. Believe the usual six day leave we have been getting every six weeks in the squadron will be cut down soon and we go back to peace timetable just when they could afford to make the leave more often. Perhaps the idea is to make everyone so cheesed off they will volunteer for the East. There was an item in the Newzie paper printed for us over here, that things had not been finalised yet, so not to bother Halifax House, so the best policy will be to sit tight and not stick one's neck out in the meantime.

The latest news exposed yet more signs of Jim's frustration with the New Zealand government:

May 24th 1945: *All the Aussies have been withdrawn from crews on the squadron and are going home very soon before being posted to the East. The Wing Co. seems hopeful that they will do the same with us too, but knowing what our government is like, I am not too sure.*

Seems that we will be eligible for a couple of ribbons – the 1939-45 Spam ribbon and the France and Germany one. Perhaps the Defence one too. Can you imagine me?

Received a photo from Bill Mallon today, taken just after he got his pansy suit on the way to Brighton. Believe he has not left yet so he will be getting plenty cheesed off down there waiting for a boat. Still we are not doing much here.

Did I mention that our new skipper Eric Butler is now a Flight-Lieutenant? He was like Bill, only a Flight- Sergeant when he arrived here last Sept, only acting rank though. Eric was actually 'Flying Officer Butler' when he was posted to Mepal and it was on the 6th October 1944. He had completed one tour already, back in 1941.

We were on battle order for an exodus trip today – that's P.O.W.s from France - but it was scrubbed. We are back on the list again and as a result had to have a jab today, the first of a series three over three weeks against infection.

We get an egg once or twice a week plus the one when we do a trip. I'm missing the chocolate flying rations we used to get and don't now.

May 29th 1945: *Today, Tuesday, we were down for some air firing out to sea, but after waiting about for three quarters of an hour and nearly lunchtime and no sign of our kite returning from another trip, Eric had it* *scrubbed. We are down tomorrow for some practice bombing in the afternoon so we may get off if we are lucky. It is the start of a group competition. Our squadron holds the cup at present. Shorty Baxter and co are now on leave prior to being posted to another squadron for the Far East…*

There was a note in Sunday's papers, I think it was, that Nash has declared NZ is bringing back twenty thousand Army chaps from overseas. (Walter Nash, the New Zealand finance minister and deputy prime minister) *That will make a big hole in the division. The chappie today was asked why the Aussies and the Canucks could withdraw all their chaps and the reply was - they pay their air force chaps themselves whereas the R.A.F. pays us and not NZ!! What the hell did NZ do?*

Tomorrow we are down again in the detail for an exodus trip – P.O.W.s from France – but so far we have been on about four times but have not done one of them – all scrubbed. Had a second jab yesterday so have got a sore wing today, in case we bring any lice back with us (probably a typhus jab).

On June 5th 1945, Jim wrote a letter in which he described taking part in a 'Baedeker' operation, or a 'Trolley mission' as the Americans called them - or even a 'Cook's Tour' as Jim called them. These were flights over some of the squadron's bombing targets to view the extent of the damage inflicted.

The squadron has started running Cook's Tours' Trips now. Two crews a day make a low level tour of the main bombed cities in Germany. We'll be able to see some of our handiwork. Takes about six hours so you can see it covers a trip of about twelve hundred miles base to base.

Yesterday, Tuesday, we were lucky enough to get our turn on one of the Cook's Tours or Baedeker trips as they are now called. The part that narked us was that we were called at six and then did not leave until about quarter to four in the afternoon. We took some bods from Bomber Command as passengers. This is where we went:

- *First to **Walcheren Island** on the Dutch coast where the dyke was breached to flood the island and trap the Germans. It was done, as the Wing*

Co said 'by 75 assisted by the RAF'. Some snobs aren't we? There is very little of the place left above the sea with the exception of the town of **Flushing***.*

- *Then across Belgium to* **Munchen Gladbach***, well damaged.*
- *Then to* **Cologne** *where by the main bridge across the Rhine the cathedral is the only large building left mainly intact, if knocked about. The city has had a real bashing.* (see aerial photograph below)
- *From there across several towns in the Ruhr as far as* **Hamm***, which was one of the places we had visited ourselves. Then back to* **Dortmund***, on past* **Gelsenkirchen***, another of our targets, to* **Essen***. That city is just dead. You may have heard and read about the damage done to the Krupp*

Cologne, 10th May 1945 (picture taken by James Beadling, co-pilot of the U.S.A.F. B-24 bomber, 'Wazzle Dazzle': courtesy of David Foster)

armament works there. It's not exaggerated a bit. The works themselves are just a mass of rusty twisted iron framework and most of the town centre is flat.
- *From there to* **Duisburg***, the biggest inland port in Germany.* (Duisburg is actually the biggest inland port in the world) *Every railroad bridge is down and there does not seem to be any movement on the railways. Nor could there be without considerable repairs and new rolling stock.*
- *We struck north from there to* **Wesel***, rather I should say where it was. There is just some parts of walls standing and in some places just a flattened mass of rubble. You will remember my mentioning we bombed several times through full*

cloud cover, by instruments as the papers called it. This place is an indication of the accuracy and concentration obtained.

- *On the way back we passed near **Nijmegen** and **Arnheim**. I got Eric to turn off to see the first but by that time he was too tired to go as far as **Arnheim**. There are still many wrecked gliders lying round in the fields there.* (They will have been there since the battle in September 1944)
- *Took us just over four hours. If we had gone in the morning we would have been able to have gone up to **Bremen** and **Hamburg** too.*

The possibility of having to continue operations in the Far East against Japan was obviously something that continued to prey on Jim's mind, having already seen several of his comrades transferred to 'Tiger Force' squadrons:

June 10th: *Did I mention that they have started to make this a fully Newzie squadron? There are plenty of guesses as to why but your guess is probably as good as mine. That reminds me too, my warrant will be due in October. That's when I can wear a flat top.* (A reference to the probability of him being awarded a commission and the cap he would wear as an officer) *If I'd been in the squadron somewhat over a month earlier, I would probably have had enough ops in to be recommended for something else. No chance here now but I'd rather return as I am than go east just for that.*

Much to Jim's relief, 'Tiger Force' was not needed. The war in the east ended a week after the Americans dropped the second atomic bomb on Nagasaki, the Japanese surrendering on the 15th August 1945. 'Tiger Force' was officially disbanded on October 31st.

Jim returned to New Zealand in November, having been promoted to the rank of Warrant Officer, and began the slow process of re-building his relationship with Sally and their two girls, Ruth and Maryann. The family had one more addition in 1948 when Penny was born. Although he did not talk about the war itself, their dad was a very patient teacher when outdoors and talking about cloud formations and the night sky, things the family came to understand had been of great importance to him in his role as a navigator.

Ruth is convinced, however, that his experiences had taken their

Jim, aged 18, front left – one of his many sporting interests before the war

toll. Although his clients always found him charming, she said that after the war he could be very morose within the family and had a fairly short fuse.

Before the war, Jim had always had wide sporting interests and had been active in competitive rifle shooting and ice hockey and had enjoyed sailing his own B Class yacht out of Lyttelton harbour, near Christchurch. He picked up where he left off when he returned home and became very active in athletics as parent, coach, timekeeper and steward. His ability to compute in his head got him to high levels in New Zealand Athletics, both at local and national level, and he was the Anemometer Steward, or Timekeeper, at the Commonwealth Games in Christchurch in 1974.

He continued to play golf and bowls throughout his life and became a keen gardener, growing dahlias and chrysanthemums for national shows and florists, and he served as chairman of his local horticultural society. He continued working as an accountant for over sixty years, only retiring as he approached eighty so that he could enjoy family events and his dachshund dog.

Ruth is not aware of Jim keeping in touch with any of his comrades from the Mallon crew after the war, but he did remain quite close to two of his fellow navigators, Neville 'String' Staples, from Bill Evenden's crew, who was from Christchurch, and Ken 'Dazzy' Dalzell from Ernest Amohanga's crew. He will have spent considerably more time training with them than he did on operations with his own crew. Another Kiwi who probably kept in touch was Randal Springer, who was posted to Mepal with the Milsom crew on the same day as the Mallon crew. Apparently Randal and 'Dazzy' remained close after the war, 'Dazzy' eventually becoming godparent to Randal's daughter.

In 2013, Ruth wrote that she had recently found Jim's name at Masterton airfield on a board of local people who served and trained there during the war. Jim had often said that it was ironic that he trained there for a while then returned twenty years later to work. During his last years he was confined to bed and he died on the 30th January 2001, just after his 90th birthday. He is buried in the Riverside Cemetery at Masterton.

Jim's and Sally's memorial stone in Masterton

10 DENIS EYNSTONE: 'TAIL-END CHARLIE'

Denis, after his promotion to Flight Sergeant.

During the long hot summer of 1940, a fifteen year-old boy sat in a field on the outskirts of Oxford and watched the aerial duels unfolding in the sky above him. Denis Eynstone observed the Battle of Britain with a mixture of excitement and horror as the Hurricanes, the Spitfires and the Messerschmitt Bf 109s fought for supremacy and he dreamt of one day playing his part.

He wasn't alone. The British public had become enthralled and the Daily Mirror had published 'Spot them in the Air', a booklet containing drawings of twenty seven British and German aircraft. Denis was

inspired and started to compile what he called his 'War Plane Atlas', made up of his own pencil drawings of aircraft from WW1 and WW2.

Two years later, when he enlisted in the R.A.F.V.R., he would have had very little idea what to expect when he eventually became an air gunner in a Lancaster bomber, and even less about the challenges faced by 'Tail-end Charlie', the name by which the rear gunner was known. His role was to be a lookout, to warn the pilot if he needed to take evasive action and to defend the aircraft from enemy fighters using his four Browning .303 inch machine guns.

The temperature at 20,000 feet can reach as low as -40°C and, although rear gunners were provided with electrically heated underwear, socks and gloves, these were not always reliable and frost bite was not uncommon. His daughter Wendy remembers her dad commenting on how desperately cold it was and said she couldn't imagine how men were able to function at such temperatures. But the cold wasn't the only problem.

Once he had squeezed himself into the tiny space inside the rear turret, he would spend up to eight and a half

An exhibit at the Yorkshire Air Museum showing a Lancaster rear gunner in his turret

hours flying backwards in cramped, freezing and solitary conditions, feeling every movement of the aircraft amplified by his position so far back. The preferred directions of attack of enemy fighters was from the rear or from beneath, so it is not surprising that the life expectancy of a rear gunner was short, estimated earlier in the war as only two weeks, or five operations. Nor is it surprising that many rear gunners reported feeling *'a bit flak happy'* afterwards, probably the early signs of post-traumatic stress disorder.

The sense of isolation felt by a rear gunner is captured perfectly in this poem, written by an unknown gunner. It was published in Adam Forrest's blog 'broodyswar.wordpress.com', created in memory of his grandfather, who was a Mosquito navigator with No. 488(NZ) Squadron, the same squadron in which Tom Mallon served.

Bumping down the runway
with the turret on the beam,
flashing past well-wishers
lit by the Drem's[4] dull gleam.

The pulling of the stomach
as we slowly climb on track,
setting course to eastward –
how many will come back?

The clipped command to alter course
as we cross the Anglian shore,
then extinguish navigation lights
As the engines increase their roar.

The throbbing of the engines
disturbs the fading light
as onward, ever onward
we fly into the night.

Routine settles to a rhythm
and those 'up front' dictate
the course, the speed, the height
and the passage of our fate.

Searching ever searching,
the turret turns to and fro,
looking, always looking
for our enemy and foe.

---

[4] *This refers to the 'Drem Lighting System' devised by the Station Commander of R.A.F. Drem in Scotland, Wing Commander (later Air Marshall) Richard Atcherley. It was developed to overcome visibility problems when landing.*

The sound of throbbing engines
envelopes our immediate night
and the clammy taste of oxygen
as I adjust the dull ring sight.

A quiet statement from the Nav -
'Enemy coast ahead',
the blood flows quicker thro' the veins,
our training stifles the dread.

Searching ever searching
for that darker smudge of black,
looking for the fighter
that could stop us getting back.

The Nav again is heard to say
'Target dead ahead'.
The tightening of the stomach
is the only sign of dread.

As a lonely, cold rear gunner
I always face the rear
and never see the target
'til the aircraft's there.

Flying ever closer, closer
to that awful scene,
every nerve is strung so tight
you stifle the need to scream.

The observer⁵ now takes full control
and by his directed call
keeps the tingling nerves on edge
'til he lets the bomb load fall.

---

⁵ *Until mid-1943 'Air Observers' were trained in both navigation and bomb-aiming and wore a brevet bearing the letter 'O'*

With the sudden upward lift
we all expect the worst,
but heave a sigh of intense relief
as the aircraft changes course.

Nose well down and increased speed
to escape from that dreadful sight
we race across the crimson sky
to the safety of the night.

As those up front now search the sky
for the fighter that lurks in the dark
while I at last see the target fires,
where we have left our mark.

'It sent shivers down my spine' was Wendy's response on reading the poem. She recently told me she had been reading *'Bomber Command'* by Max Hastings and it made her '... *realise just how terrifying it must have been for those young men and just how lucky we are to be here'.*

When she responded to my letter in 2014, she knew very little about her dad's war service or what he had done in the years following the war, but she was able to provide me with some fascinating photographs. These raised more questions than they answered, though, as none of the pictures appeared to be of No. 75(NZ) Squadron. One of them was clearly taken in Italy and one had what appeared to be a U.S. B29 Superfortress bomber in the background.

Wendy was very keen to fill in the gaps, not only for me but, more importantly, for herself and her two sons. She acquired Denis' service record from the R.A.F. at Cranwell and the story gradually emerged. Despite the difficulties he'd experienced as a rear gunner, Denis was a young man who clearly found life in the R.A.F. quite appealing. Not only did he stay on longer than any of the other members of the crew, but his dissatisfaction with civilian life after the war led to his re-enlisting four years later.

None of the Mallon crew was more suited to life in the air force than Denis, with his experience as a teenager in the Air Training Corps and his passion for aircraft, and it's not surprising that he was in no hurry to return to his job as a clerk when the war ended. It took Wendy and me some time to solve the mysteries thrown up by her dad's photographs, but the details of what he did after the war gradually became clearer.

On the **21st July 1945**, when the squadron moved to R.A.F. Spilsby, Denis remained at Mepal and joined No. 44 (Rhodesia) Squadron, which moved in the opposite direction. Both squadrons at this stage were preparing to join 'Tiger Force' to continue the war against Japan, but when the Japanese surrendered a few weeks later Denis found himself with a new challenge, 'Operation Dodge'.

This involved large numbers of Lancasters flying to Italy in the autumn of 1945 to help with the repatriation of soldiers of the 8th Army, some of whom had been away from home for five or six years fighting in North Africa and Italy. One of the pick-up airfields was R.A.F. Pomigliano, near Naples, which explains the photograph of Denis in warm weather uniform in front of a building labelled 'R.A.F. *Pomigliano C.M.F.* (Central Mediterranean Forces) *Terminal Building*'.

One of the attractions was a sight-seeing trip to Pompeii, in the

Denis, on the right, relaxing in the sun at R.A.F. Pomigliano

shadow of Mount Vesuvius, which had erupted the previous year, its last major eruption. We will never know if Denis took advantage of the opportunity but, whilst researching the Pomigliano connection, I came across this account on the BBC's 'WW2 People's War' website:

After the European and Far Eastern hostilities were finished an interesting operation called 'Operation Dodge' was instigated. This was the means of using a huge fleet of Lancaster Bombers and the attendant aircrews who were now 'out of a job' in order to transport soldiers of the 8th Army back home from holding units in Italy - especially those who had been away from home for 4-5 years.

My third trip out on October 8th was to Pomigliano near Naples, with Mount Vesuvius on the landing circuit, which looked quite menacing - as at that time clouds of smoke were still being given out after the major eruption in 1944. The day after the landing was considered a rest day and was spent visiting the ruins of Pompeii, which at the time was considered a great experience and not to be missed.

On each occasion we returned with 20 soldier passengers on board who were delighted to be going home in a few hours instead of a few weeks by sea, regardless of the discomfort, noise of 4 Merlins and sometimes air sickness.

So the aircraft specially built to carry bombs and destroy cities were at the last used for a more humanitarian reason and the aircrew who flew in them were given a pleasant job to carry out and at the same time have a mini holiday. It was a very rewarding experience and a memory to cherish.

A matter of interest to the modern traveller - the trip out was 14-15 hours - much different to today's travel by jet liner!!

Whilst with No. 44 Squadron, Denis was awarded the 'Good Conduct Badge' in recognition of three years' service and was then promoted to flight sergeant. The squadron re-located to R.A.F. Wyton, also in Cambridgeshire, in **1946** then, from September to January the following year, he had postings with No. 90 Squadron at R.A.F. Tuddenham in Suffolk and then a month at back in Cambridgeshire at R.A.F. Oakington, until his service came to an end on the **19th January 1947**. He was officially 'released' on the **17th March**, but he would be back in uniform just over four years later when he re-enlisted on the 28th August 1951

Wendy, who was not born until 1958, knows very little about what her dad did during those years in civilian life, other than marry her mum Winifred in 1950, and, until she acquired his service record in 2015, she was unaware that he had re-enlisted.

On the **4th September 1951**, he was posted to No. 230 O.C.U. (Operational Conversion Unit) at R.A.F. Lindholme in South Yorkshire where he became acclimatised once more to life in the air force and in **December** he joined No. 7 Squadron at R.A.F. Upwood, yet another air base in Cambridgeshire.

No. 7 Squadron was equipped with Avro Lincolns at the time, the R.A.F.'s front-line bomber in the Cold War, but after just four months Denis was transferred to the squadron with which he would serve the longest period, No. 35 Squadron. Having been disbanded in February 1950, the squadron was re-formed on the 1st September 1951 at R.A.F. Marham, Norfolk, and equipped with the Boeing Washington. Marham became the Conversion Unit for the Washington, the aircraft previously known as the B29 Superfortress, which had the dubious distinction of being the aircraft

Denis, back row, 2nd from right, in front of a No. 35 Squadron Boeing Washington, 1952

that dropped the atomic bombs on Hiroshima and Nagasaki.

Denis stayed with the squadron as a gunner for the next two years and Wendy recalls Denis telling her that a number of his friends who had flown in these *'worn-out planes'* had lost their lives when they crashed. Records show that the squadron lost two of these aircraft whilst Denis was at Marham, although there were others lost by other squadrons during the same period. The No. 35 Squadron B29s lost were:

> **WF570,** which crashed near Swaffham, five miles north east of Marham, on 14th December 1952. Both its pilots, the navigator and the radio operator were killed, whilst the flight engineer and one of the gunners were seriously injured. The crash was put down to a fuel leak or a missing fuel cap.
>
> **WF495,** which crashed in the Irish Sea just after midnight on the 26th January 1954 as a result of severe icing. It was being returned to the United States and was en route from R.A.F. Prestwick via the Azores. A distress call was received and several lifeboats were launched, but they recovered none of the crew of seven who were believed to have bailed out. The body of one of them was subsequently recovered by the crew of a trawler.

Denis was at all times a loyal and conscientious member of the R.A.F. but Wendy recalled a story that demonstrated that he was also fiercely independent and had a well-developed sense of right and wrong. He had told her of an incident, whilst with No. 35 Squadron, when a bomb became frozen to its mounting in extreme weather conditions and the pilot, considered by several members of the crew to be rather reckless, told Denis to kick it free. Denis was, to say the least, reluctant to do so and, after the exchange of some expletives in which he described what should be done, he was proved correct and the bomb fell into the sea as it thawed out at lower altitude

Unaware of her dad's post war record, Wendy had thought the story came from his time with No. 75(NZ) Squadron, but when she gave me the pilot's name it turned out to be his pilot at No. 35 Squadron. Two months after Denis finally left the R.A.F. two one thousand pound bombs fell off a trolley at R.A.F. Marham and exploded on the runway, killing one man and badly damaging several aircraft. Denis was right to be cautious.

On the **22nd March 1954**, Denis left the squadron and was posted to the School of Maritime Reconnaissance at R.A.F. St. Mawgan in Cornwall, where he was re-united with the Lancaster bomber, now being used as a reconnaissance aircraft. He stayed there for about seven weeks before being discharged from the R.A.F. for the last time on the **10th July**. According to his service record and the 'Queen's Regulations/Air Council Instructions' for 1954, the reason for his discharge was that he was *'Below the standard for pilot, etc.'* Did Denis still harbour aspirations to be a pilot?

Having returned to civilian life, Denis became a fitter at the pressed steel car plant in Oxford and, in 1958, Winifred gave birth to their daughter Wendy. In 1960, Denis became a successful self-employed builder and, when he retired in 1987, he and Winifred moved to Hartland in north Devon where they had many happy years.

The sketch Wendy found among her dad's belongings

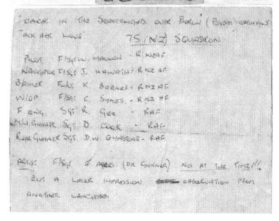

As well as the service record and the photographs, Wendy also sent me some fascinating mementoes from her dad's belongings. The first was a sketch of the Mallon crew's Lancaster, apparently on the Potsdam operation of April 14th 1945. The caption explains that the artist drew it sometime after the operation and, apart from the misspelling of my dad's name, there are a number of questions raised by the picture:

- Who was the artist? There was a Flight Sergeant Ayres with the squadron in 1941 but not in 1945. When did he draw it and why that particular operation?

- Artistic licence may explain why the aircraft is AA-L, which was not involved in the Potsdam operation, but why is the bomb aimer named as F/L K. Barnes? There was a replacement bomb aimer on that operation because of Ken Philp's ankle injury but, according to the O.R.B., it was Owen Willetts.

Despite these questions, the drawing remains a valuable piece of memorabilia, as does the collection of pencil drawings made by Denis in 1940 in his own 'War Plane Atlas'.

Denis died in 2011 at the age of eighty six and, although he rarely spoke about the war years, Wendy passed on a couple of stories that provided an insight into the feelings that he kept buried for so many years after the war. Towards the end of his life, Denis confided in the manager of his care home that '*I have been a bad man.*' When questioned later about what he meant by this, he explained it was because of the bombing of German towns and cities and the inevitable deaths of so many innocent people, including women and children.

Denis was certainly not alone in feeling guilty for the part he played in the war. Bob shared his concern, and to this day the policy of 'Area bombing' remains one of the great controversies of the Second World War. As Wendy pointed out in her letter to me, '*without any recognition or help for post-traumatic stress syndrome these men must have carried these thoughts to the grave.*'

In 2005, at the age of eighty, Denis was involved in a serious road accident and was trapped in his car. He described having a wartime flashback to an incident when the aircraft was hit by flak and he was trapped in his turret, unable to reach his 'chute, as fuel ran through the aircraft. The aircraft landed on the grass alongside the runway to reduce the risk of fire and Denis was hauled out by the ground crew, having thought that he would not get out alive.

It is interesting to compare his recollection of the episode with that of Bill, who said in his interview *'the flak went through the oil (cooler) core ...one engine is not a big loss on a Lancaster,'* or Bob, who simply wrote in his log book *'port inner feathered - hit by flak'*. What may seem like a lack of concern for the feelings of the rear gunner may just be a lack of awareness amongst a group of men who all had their own anxieties to deal with.

Part of Denis Eynstone's 'War Plane Atlas'.

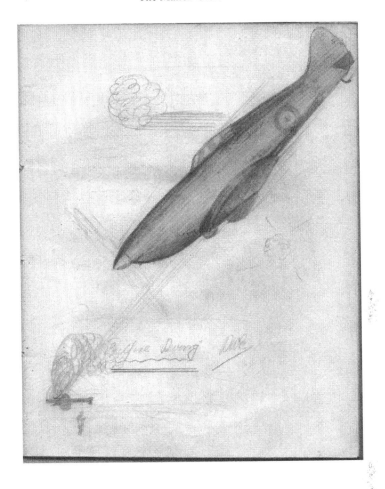

11 THE REST OF THE CREW: 'AN O.M.G. MOMENT'

Frank Symes, trainee wireless operator, 1943

Jim Haworth wasn't the only one facing worrying uncertainty in the months following V.E Day. Although peace had come to Europe, for those fighting or incarcerated in the Far East the bloodshed continued and the four Kiwis still in the Mallon crew, as well as Ken and Denis, who were now in other squadrons, were all expecting to have to join that brutal struggle. Despite its exotic title, 'Tiger Force' was something that all the New Zealand and Australian forces serving in Europe were dreading.

At the Quebec Conference of September 1944, Winston Churchill had proposed the transfer of between five hundred and a thousand heavy bombers from Bomber Command to the Pacific once Germany was defeated. U.S. President Franklin D. Roosevelt had enthusiastically accepted the offer, warning that a *'long and costly struggle'* still lay ahead.

By the end of the war the proposed force, nicknamed 'Tiger Force', had been scaled back to ten squadrons from Britain, Canada, Australia and New Zealand. It was to be based on Okinawa, flying Avro Lancasters, Avro Lincolns and Consolidated Liberators.

The squadrons eventually allocated to the force were:

- R.A.F. Nos. 7, **9** (Ken Philp's squadron), 35, **44** (Denis Eynstone's squadron), 49, **75(NZ)** (Eric, Frank, Jim and Lance) 207, 617, 627, 635 and 692.

- R.C.A.F. Nos. 405, 408, 419, 420, 425, 428, 431, 434 and, as a Support Unit, No. 426 (Transport)

- R.A.A.F. Nos. 460, 463 and 467.

Frank (17) just before enlisting

Following the surrender of the Japanese in August 1945, and much to the relief of those posted to 'Tiger Force' squadrons, the force was officially disbanded two months later. One of those who welcomed the news was **Frank Symes,** who had continued after V.E. Day as Eric Butler's Wireless Operator. He was repatriated to New Zealand in December 1945 and demobbed in March 1946, before returning to the Wairoa district. He eventually moved to the Mahia Peninsula, where he was employed by the Mahia Freight Company.

He met Winnie Smith, who had moved to New Zealand from Fiji when she was seventeen, while she was working at the Morere Tearooms, just north of Nuhaka. They married in November 1954 and settled in Wairoa, where Frank took on a job at the local freezing works and later at the Deluxe Ford gas service station. The couple went on to have seven children, six sons and one daughter, Stuart, Yvonne, Graeme, John, Anthony, Stephen and Cecil.

On the 26th February 2015, Barrie Mallon sent me an e-mail after reading my blog post about Frank. We began to doubt our assumption that none of the crew had been in contact after the war.

Hi Vic,

You have just given me an O.M.G. moment!!

I have just read about Frank Symes and it mentions about Frank meeting Winnie at the Morere tea rooms.

Well, the tearooms have a long history in our family as when we were young and lived in Gisborne our annual bank holiday was to Morere and the tearooms camping ground which, looking at their website, has not changed since we were there which would have been in the early to mid-1960s.

We and our friends from across the road in Gisborne would pack up our caravans and spend the long weekend there, the thermal hot springs are the attraction.

It mentions that Frank worked for the Deluxe Ford gas service station and as dad was a travelling salesman for a car spare parts and accessories firm in Gisborne his calling area would have been to Nuhaka and Wairoa - so he must have had contact with Frank.

Regards,

Barrie.

Frank died on the 4th November 1979 at the age of fifty five, coincidentally the same age at which Bob had died five years earlier, and is buried at the Wairoa Cemetery next to his mother, Ellen. He is survived by Winnie, six of his children and twenty six grandchildren. Winnie and Yvonne, Warren's mum, still live in the Wairoa district, as do two of Frank's sons, Graeme and John, and daughter-in-law Pauline, wife of the late Stuart.

Like so many of the Mallon crew, Frank's family was touched by tragedy, albeit many years after the war. On the 11th February 2012, Frank and Winnie's eldest son Stuart, who ran a fish and chip shop in Nuhaka in the Hawke's Bay region, was killed in a car accident near Morere at the age of fifty six. According to the local newspaper he was *'one of Nuhaka's best known and loved residents.'*

No. 9 Squadron was based at R.A.F. Bardney in Lincolnshire until the 7th July 1945, and was one of the squadrons allocated to Tiger Force.

When **Ken Philp** left Mepal on the 15th June and was transferred to Bardney, he did so with some trepidation. However, instead of embarking on another phase of the war, which he had been expecting, he had an altogether much happier experience when he met his future wife, Marjorie, and her daughter Joan, in nearby Lincoln.

In the late summer of 1945, an amazing twist of fate took Ken to Trieste in Italy. His squadron was taking part in 'Operation Dodge', the operation in which Denis was involved, returning soldiers who had been fighting in North Africa and Italy. There, he met up with his brother Jack who was waiting with the 2nd New Zealand Division, commonly known as 'the Div', for transport home.

The Italian campaign had been New Zealand's primary combat contribution to the war following the hard-won victory over Axis forces in North Africa. Almost all the New Zealanders who served in Italy did so as members of 'the Div' and they had endured harsh winters and eighteen months of gruelling combat before ending the war in Trieste, in May 1945. The legacy of the campaign was profound and long-lasting, with more than 2,100 New Zealanders killed and 6,700 wounded during the liberation of Italy. Limited availability of shipping and the political chaos that followed the German surrender meant that the evacuation of New Zealand troops would prove a slow process and it was not until February 1946 that the last Kiwis left.

The brothers' joy at meeting up in Trieste would have been diminished by the sadness they felt about their younger brother 'Gibb', who had lost his life eighteen months earlier in France. F/O Gibson Philp, pictured over the page, had been a pilot with No. 486(NZ) Squadron based at R.A.F. Tangmere in West Sussex since September 1943. Equipped with the Hawker Typhoon, the squadron had become a ground attack unit targeting shipping and airfields in France and providing escort missions for R.A.F. and U.S.A.A.F. light and medium daylight bombers.

In 1944, the squadron was involved in what were known as 'Ramrod' operations, short range bomber attacks to destroy ground targets in France. On the 14th January, Gibson was involved in operation 'Ramrod 453', in which British and American aircraft attempted to destroy German flying bomb sites near Fruges in the Pas de Calais region of northern France.

Raids on these sites were notoriously difficult, with very strong anti-aircraft fire, targets well-camouflaged, the majority with no conspicuous landmarks, and information on the exact position of each site often unreliable. Add to that the problems caused by the winter weather, and losses were very high. Gibson's Typhoon Mk IB SA-R (JR329) was hit by flak whilst flying at low altitude and he had little chance of survival. He was just twenty three years old and left a young wife, Nancy. He is buried in the Viroflay New Communal Cemetery in Yvelines, just outside Paris.

Ken and Jack eventually returned to their family, parents Ralph and Maud and sister Enid, in New Zealand. Ken maintained a long distance relationship with Marjorie for several years until she eventually left her home in Lincoln and joined him in New Zealand. They married in the early 1950s, and for most of his working life Ken was employed as a sheet metal worker by Chubb, in Porirua. He died on the 13th June 1991 at the age of seventy seven and is buried in the Whenua Tapu Cemetery in Pukerua Bay, Porirua.

Eric Butler was also expecting to continue active service when the war in Europe ended, and he too was relieved when he was provided with transport home on the 28th September 1945, just over a month after the Japanese surrender. He was born on New Year's Eve 1917 in Wellington, and was twenty seven when he took over the Mallon crew. He had already completed his first tour with the squadron in 1941 when it was based at Feltwell and equipped with Wellington bombers and had been posted to Mepal for his second tour on the 6th October 1944.

His new crew then had quite a baptism of fire as Eric took them on nine operations, including raids on Stuttgart, Flushing, Essen, Leverkusen, Cologne and Castrop-Rauxel.

According to one of Jim's letters, Eric then had to stop flying and spent the first few months of 1945 in hospital, seeing no more action until he took a crew on an operation to Bremen on the 22nd April 1945. Three days later he took charge of the Mallon crew.

Eric was living in Levin, in the Manawatu-Wanganui region of the North Island, when he died on the 26th of July 1994 at the age of seventy six. His ashes are buried in the Avenue Cemetery in Levin.

Lancelot Waugh was not transferred to No. 9 squadron with the rest of his crew in June 1945, remaining instead at Mepal and replacing Ken Philp as the Mallon crew's bomb aimer. I learnt more about Lance's crew, the Milson crew, during e-mail exchanges with Keith Springer, the son of Randal Springer, its wireless operator. Randal had written some notes in the 1990s about his war-time experiences and, in December 2013, Keith discovered they included reference to the transfer of his crew immediately after the war:

Having completed some successful operations over Germany our crew was considered sufficiently experienced to become part of a specialist squadron in the offensive against Japan and we were posted to No 9 Squadron at R.A.F. Bardney, Lincolnshire, which was a few miles east of the city of Lincoln. We were now ...part of what became known as 'Tiger Force'. ... On 6 July we flew to our new base at Waddington, the Dam Buster base a few miles south of Lincoln. We shared the base with 617 Sqdn so there were two very well-known RAF squadrons together.

Waddington had actually only been home to No. 617 Squadron for about three weeks when No. 9 Squadron arrived, and neither would stay there very long. Previously, 617 had been based at R.A.F. Scampton, from where it took part in the 'Dam Buster' raids, and then at R.A.F. Woodhall Spa.

Lance was born in Taranaki in 1914, just before the outbreak of the First World War, and married Hazel just before setting off for training in Canada. Hazel died on the 11th March 1943, just a couple of weeks after waving goodbye to Lance. She was just twenty six years old. It would be more than two years before Lance was able to return to New Zealand after being demobbed in July 1945.

Nine years later, whilst furthering his education, Lance published 'The Historical Development of Kowhai Intermediate School' for his thesis at the University of Auckland. He completed his M.A. in 1955 and died in 1994 at the age of eighty.

Owen Willetts, Ken Philp's replacement bomb aimer for the 14th April operation when Ken was incapacitated, was twenty three and had completed twenty one operations with F/S Murray Smith's crew between July and October 1944. He had then been transferred to No. 291 Squadron and, on the 28th March 1945, he was re-posted to No. 75(NZ) Squadron.

Owen, pictured below with his 'Observer' brevet clearly visible, was born on the 27th February 1922 and was living in Burke's Pass in South Canterbury when he died in 1994 at the age of seventy one. In July 2015, more than ten years after his death, the 'Timaru Herald' published an article about Owen. His family had donated a number of his belongings to the South Canterbury Aviation Heritage Centre, which had set up a new display. The article described the display as follows:

The new section within the complex, called 'They Served with Honour', will house several exhibitions and displays specific to the South Canterbury area.

One of those will feature paraphernalia from the late WWII veteran, Owen Willetts of Burke's Pass. Willetts was a navigator in the New Zealand 75th Squadron and flew Lancaster Bombers.

A display based on his material, including photographs, maps, and notes relating to bombing raids over Europe, will demonstrate precision bombing techniques. His original flying suit made of leather complete with boots and jacket adds to the reality of the exhibition.

Charles Green D.F.C., who had re-trained as a mid-under gunner in 1945, flew on only three operations with the Mallon crew and probably spoke hardly a word to my dad but, on the 1st March 2016, I received an e-mail that was to signal one of the most significant events of my four years of research:

Hi there, my name is Mike Cleary, I have a friend who is mentioned in the crew of your father's historic records of 75 NZ Sqdn.

His name is Charles Frederick Green D.F.C. (mid under gunner). I am trying to find out how I might get a copy of his citation for the D.F.C. he was awarded. He has no knowledge of a U.K. based association which might help...can you?

He is a fabulous chap who wouldn't have done this himself but I think he deserves some recognition of his wartime experiences.

Hoping you can help......Mike C.

I provided Mike with the information he required and, within two weeks, I was speaking on the 'phone to the only surviving member of my dad's crew, one of a dwindling number of men who had served with Bomber Command. He was articulate, his memory was excellent and he left me reflecting on what my dad's premature death had denied us.

When Charles was posted to Mepal in January 1945, he had already completed one tour with No. 429 Squadron, where this picture was taken. He arrived with another gunner, P/O Gwyn Duglan, from R.A.F. Feltwell, the home of No. 3 Lancaster Finishing School.

He was born in Peckham, the home of fictional 'heroes' Del and Rodney Trotter, in October 1921. The family escaped the urban sprawl of south east London in 1930 by moving out to what was then the rural haven of Dagenham, in Essex, and Charles eventually attended the newly opened Eastbrook Senior Boys' School. After leaving school in 1935, he worked for a commercial printer in London and has vivid memories of the delays he and his father experienced travelling in to work during the Blitz.

He volunteered to join the air force in January 1941 while he was still only nineteen and, while waiting for his call-up, attended the local Technical College to pursue further education. He was accepted by the R.A.F.V.R. but had to wait a full twelve months before being called up in January 1942. There followed more than eighteen months of training, including a spell at the Air Gunnery School at R.A.F. Dalcross in Inverness where, a year later, Denis Eynstone would spend three months.

In September 1943, he was posted to No. 429 Squadron at R.A.F. Leeming in North Yorkshire, coincidentally the same squadron where S/L Alban Chipling had been awarded the D.F.C. earlier that year. After his first operation on Christmas Eve 1943, Charles went on to complete thirty four operations as a Halifax mid-upper gunner before becoming 'tour expired' in July 1944. He then had *'a fairly easy time of it'* for five months, taking long leaves and carrying out routine jobs on the base before being recalled to R.A.F. Feltwell in December.

At Feltwell, he was trained in the use of the larger 0.50 calibre machine guns and the mid-under gun turret before being posted to R.A.F. Mepal in January 1945 for his second tour. Whilst at R.A.F. Mepal, Charles completed sixteen more operations, flying with any crew that happened to be assigned to one of the Lancasters fitted with a mid-under turret. The O.R.B. suggests there were about twelve of these in the squadron, but all of Charles' sixteen operations were in the same aircraft, AA-L (HK562), with at least nine different crews. It is not surprising that he doesn't remember anyone from that period, apart from Marjorie.

Charles had met Marjorie, who worked in the Officers' Mess, shortly after arriving at Mepal and they continued seeing each other after the war. In March 2016, Chris Newey sent me a picture he had discovered in a book written by Grant Alan Russell D.F.C., *'Dying for Democracy'*. Both Chris and I thought we recognised Marjorie from a photograph of the couple that Mike Cleary had sent me and, sure enough, Mike was able to confirm that our identification was correct.

In July 1945, Charles was sent on an 'admin course' and there followed a series of administrative jobs at R.A.F. Coningsby and R.A.F.

Staff of the Officers' Mess at R.A.F. Mepal, 1945. Marjorie is 2nd from the right.
(picture: Grant Alan Russell D.F.C.)

Padgate, including interviewing personnel prior to 'demob' and later taking charge of his own 'flight' of new recruits undergoing basic training.

Marjorie lived with her parents in the village of Dore, near Sheffield, and, when Charles was demobbed, he found work as a printer with the Sheffield Star. They married in 1947 and the four of them continued to live in the old cottage in Dore, which was gradually becoming more and more dilapidated. In 1960, after a holiday in Blackpool, they decided that a move to a newer house by the seaside would benefit them all. Charles applied successfully for a job at the Blackpool Evening Gazette and they all moved to Poulton-le-Fylde, to the house in which Charles still lives.

When V.E. Day cut short his second tour, Charles had completed a total of fifty operations and, on the 25th September 1945, he was awarded the Distinguished Flying Cross. When I spoke to him on the 'phone in 2016, he insisted that he was not a hero and that he didn't want to be embarrassed by anything I wrote about him. He *'was only doing what everyone else was doing. We all did our bit'* he said. I respect his wishes, of course, so I will do no more than repeat the words of his D.F.C. citation. *'This air gunner has completed numerous operations against the enemy, in the course of which he has invariably displayed the utmost fortitude, courage and devotion to duty.'*

12 JACK MALLON: 'FOR YOUR TOMORROW'

A German soldier inspects the wreckage of Jack's Bristol Blenheim, 9th October 1940
(picture courtesy of Michel Beckers)

**'When you go home, tell them of us and say,
for your tomorrow, we gave our today'**

John Maxwell Edmunds (1875 – 1958)

Jack Mallon arrived in Britain from New Zealand in July 1939, two months before his family listened on the radio to the declaration of war. There followed several weeks of strenuous training at R.A.F. Duxford in Cambridgeshire, now home to the 'Imperial War Museum Duxford' and the 'American Air Museum', before continuing his training at R.A.F. Ternhill in Shropshire. His first operational posting was to No. 53 Squadron, a Strategic Reconnaissance Unit stationed in France.

He was soon promoted to the rank of Pilot Officer and, flying a Bristol Blenheim, he took part in numerous sorties against the advancing Wehrmacht. As the squadron's losses mounted, with particularly heavy losses in the spring of 1940, it became impossible to maintain such an advanced base and the squadron re-located to the south of England. It eventually arrived at R.A.F. Detling in Kent in May 1940, becoming part of Coastal Command. From there Jack continued operations over France, including support for the evacuation of the British Expeditionary Force from the beaches of Dunkirk in May and June, 1940.

Jack is described in his school's memorial book as

That kind of teenager, a straight-shooter instinctively trusted to lend a hand and see a job finished properly.

He soon became a highly proficient pilot and it was a severe blow for the squadron when, in October 1940, he became the first of Bill's brothers to be killed.

Some of the details of his death did not emerge until many years after the war. All the Mallon family knew at the time was that his aircraft was reported missing on the 8th October 1940. It was subsequently confirmed that he had been shot down over France and all of the crew had been killed. They eventually learned that he was buried in the small French town of Guînes, alongside his crew, observer Sergeant Wilfred Philip Whetton D.F.M., and wireless operator/air gunner Sergeant Arthur Thomas Shackleford.

It is easy to say that time is a great healer, but Bill was tormented by the deaths of both his brothers for many years after the war. In January 1995, at the age of seventy five, he wrote a letter to Paul Warnault, the mayor of Guînes, in the hope of learning more about the circumstances surrounding Jack's death. He received a reply the following month and, for the first time, he discovered that Jack had actually survived the crash.

Dear Sir,

It is with a certain emotion that I received your letter that gave me a memory of the tragic and glorious destination of your brother who is sleeping in peace with us from October 8th 1944. In fact it is for 30 years now I go twice a year to say a prayer and to put flowers on the graves of the RAF pilots, this is on November 11th and May 8th. And I was always wondering, by reading the names on the graves that we hadn't had any news from their family. They are 5 Englishmen, 1 Poland and your brother. You broke the silence and I thank you for that. This will permit me to make remember on May the 8th in a special way, your brother's glorious end.

I send you hereby a copy of a book that came out after the war....in which... the writer talks about John Mallon and his death in the German Military hospital in Guînes. To situate our village I should say we are at about 10km out of Calais, a country town of 5167 people. From the beginning of July 1940 the Germans transformed the Calais area in a landing platform and our village Guînes and neighbourhood to an airport as an attack base on England - the famous 'Battle of England.'

The Germans claimed everything/ houses, barns, the Town Hall, shops, schools. That way one of our schools has been transformed in to a hospital by the means of real German organisation method.

Your brother was the only alive person coming out of the shot down Blenheim.... but he was very badly hurt when they got him out of the plane and transported to the Guînes hospital, where he died. He has been buried with other heroes of the 39-45 war. That is what I wanted to tell you as an answer to your letter of January 1995.

With my warmest greetings and my best wishes for 1995,

Le Maire de Guînes,

Paul Warnault.

Bill wrote back to Paul, thanking him for his good wishes and the information he had provided and, shortly afterwards, after Paul had attended the memorial ceremony on the 8th May, he wrote to Bill again:

Dear Sir,

I have managed to get a few photos of the 8th May ceremony at Guînes, which took place, as it does every year, in the military section of our little cemetery.

I wanted also to especially emphasise our gratitude on this 50th anniversary of the signing of the Armistice, for the allies who died for the freedom of France and of the whole world.

I have laid a tricoloured wreath on your brother's grave, and I read your letter of 13th March to the people gathered around us.

In thanking you and your family again for your sacrifice so freely given, I beg you to believe the sincerity of my feelings.

Paul Warnault.

I initially read Paul's words with some scepticism, dismissing them as overly sentimental, but when I discovered something of his experiences during the dark days of the Nazi occupation of France, any doubts I may have harboured about his sincerity quickly disappeared.

He was born in Guînes in 1923 and his father died when he was only two years old. He was seventeen when the Germans took his home town in May 1940 following the 'Siege of Calais', and attempts to join the fight alongside the retreating British troops failed and he was made to return to school. He eventually qualified as a P.E. teacher in 1943 and became actively involved in the resistance movement, later known as the Forces Francaises de l'Interieur (F.F.I.). As well as being the mayor of Guînes for three decades after the war, he also continued to make an active contribution to education, health and defence throughout his life and has received many honours.

After writing a brief biography of Paul, pictured here in 2008, I realised I had relied rather heavily on uncorroborated information from the internet so, the following year, I decided I would try to contact him so that he could correct any inaccuracies in my story. I eventually managed to find an e-mail address and sent him a link to the blog, asking if he would check what I had written.

I was delighted to receive the following reply from his son, also called Paul:

Dear Vic,

I am Paul junior and my father who is now 91 years ask me to tell you that you can use and mention his letters in your blog. I have read the chapter 13 of your blog, all is correct about him. Just a small mistake in the translation of his letters -the name of the village is GUÎNES but not GUINESS as the famous bier.

I can again tell you that he finish as Colonel in the reserve army. Find enclosed also picture of the graves of RAF pilots and airmen who rest in peace in our cemetery. These graves have always been cleaned, maintained and flowered twice a year.

As teacher, he has explained and repeated to all his pupils that they must never forget that young brave guys coming from many countries died far from home for our freedom and are buried here at Guînes.

Best wishes,

Paul Warnault

I was extremely grateful to Paul for taking the time to reply on behalf of his father and confirm the details of my story, and I know that Jack's nephews appreciate what continues to be done to keep the memory of their uncle alive. There is no doubt that there is a corner of northern France where Jack's sacrifice is not forgotten.

It is significant that, in Paul Warnault's correspondence with Bill, the date of Jack's death was given as the 8th October 1940, the date which also appears on the headstone of Jack's grave and on the Commonwealth War Graves Commission website. In 1998, a friend of Bill's, also called Jack, sent him a letter that questioned that date. It contained a passage from the book 'For Your Tomorrow' by Errol Martyn. The book, a record of New Zealanders who have died while serving with the R.N.Z.A.F. and Allied Air Services, provides more detail about Jack's death:

Tuesday, the 8th October, 1940.

Coastal Command attack on motor transport and shipping concentrations at Gravelines, France.

No. 53 Squadron from R.A.F. Detling in Kent – 16 Group.

Blenheim IV T2036 (PZ-K) took off at 1845 and brought down by flak, crashing at about 2245 near Fréthun, 5km S.W. of Calais. Two of the crew died on the day of the crash, while the pilot was seriously injured, captured and admitted to hospital at Guînes, 6km S.E. of Fréthun. He died three days later. All three airmen are buried at Guînes.

Pilot 42719 P/O John Charles Mallon R.A.F. age 24.

Friday 11th October 1940 P/O J. C. Mallon died of injuries received on the 8th.

The C.W.G.C. Register incorrectly gives date of death for Mallon as the 8th.

Brother Thomas Alexander Mallon died on the 12th March 1945 while flying with No. 488 Squadron R.N.Z.A.F.

This was a revelation for Bill, who now knew that not only had Jack survived the crash on the 8th May but that he had then been cared for in a German military hospital for three days before succumbing to his injuries on the 11th.

The letter also highlights references in the book to the number of old boys of the Mallons' former school, New Plymouth Boys' High School, who were killed whilst serving in the air force (see Chapter 14), and to a period in 1942 when No.75 (NZ) Squadron's losses were particularly bad:

Dear Bill,

Nancy P------ (?) lent me the recently published book by Errol Martyn in which he gives details of all the NZ airmen (including FAA) killed between 1915 and 1942. A further volume comes out later. I have found it interesting, especially to check the 62 NPBHS Old Boys in the record. Enclosed is his record of Jack's accident. I thought I would send it just in case you had not seen it and were not aware he had been in hospital for three days. Bill, it's still so terrible to re-read the awful cost. That black period in 1942 when 75th lost 31 men in 3 days!

Excuse my typing.

Kindest regards to you both.

Hope all is well on the health front.

Sincerely,

Jack.

Further information about Jack's crash emerged in December 2015, when I received an e-mail from Michel Beckers in the Netherlands. Michel carries out research on behalf of the website *'aircrewremembered.com'* and produces memorials to aircrew killed in action. He wanted to use some of the pictures I had posted in my blog in the memorial to Jack that he was working on. There are now memorials to both Jack and Tom Mallon on the website.

Michel also had in his possession a photograph of a badly damaged Bristol Blenheim being guarded by two German soldiers, reproduced at the beginning of this chapter,. The identifying letters on the fuselage of the aircraft are ??-K, T2036. It is clearly a photograph of Jack's aircraft, PZ-K, just hours after it was shot down.

Whilst it was some comfort to Bill to know that his brother was remembered in the town where he was buried, especially as he was thousands of miles from home, there were some aspects of his death that left him feeling very bitter indeed.

'Never was so much owed by so many to so few'

Winston Churchill (1874 – 1965)

Churchill's memorable speech in the House of Commons on August the 20th 1940 is generally thought to refer to the courageous young men who, in the Spitfires and Hurricanes of Fighter Command, took on the might of the Luftwaffe. What followed in the speech, though, is less widely known:

All hearts go out to the fighter pilots, whose brilliant actions we see with our own eyes day after day, but we must never forget that all the time, night after night, month after month, our bomber squadrons travel far into Germany, find their targets in the darkness by the highest navigational skill, aim their attacks, often under the heaviest fire, often with serious loss, with deliberate, careful discrimination, and inflict shattering blows upon the whole of the technical and war-making structure of the Nazi power. On no part of the Royal Air Force does the weight of the war fall more heavily than on the daylight bombers who will play an invaluable part in the case of invasion and whose unflinching zeal it has been necessary in the meanwhile on numerous occasions to restrain...

The rivalry between fighter pilots and bomber crews is legendary. According to Guy Gibson's memoirs, there was some resentment amongst bomber crews at the perceived hero worship for the *'scarf-flapping glamour boys'* of Fighter Command. I doubt that the three Mallon brothers would have paid much attention to such trivia, all three taking great pride in their respective roles, but there was one issue that caused a lifetime of disappointment and bitterness for Bill, 'a *festering sore... right up to his passing away'* is how Bill's son Barrie describes it.

Jack died on the 11th October 1940, after being shot down during a Coastal Command operation, and his name appears on the Battle of Britain Roll of Honour in the R.A.F. Chapel in Westminster Abbey, commemorating aircrew killed or mortally wounded in the battle. Of the one thousand four hundred and ninety seven names on the roll, four hundred and forty nine were in Fighter Command, seven hundred and thirty two were in Bomber Command, two hundred and sixty eight were in Coastal Command and the remainder in other commands and the Fleet Air Arm. Unfortunately, arguments over who should be included in *'the few'*

Jack's name on the Battle of Britain Roll of Honour in Westminster Abbey referred to in Churchill's speech resulted in a grave injustice being inflicted on many of these heroes.

The Battle of Britain Clasp, an addition to the 1939-45 Star, was awarded after the war to aircrew who had taken part in the battle between the 10th July and the 31st October 1940, but, according to the Air Ministry Orders of 1946 (A.544/1946), this award was

> *Not available for personnel who flew in aircraft other than fighters, notwithstanding that they may have engaged with the enemy during the qualifying period.*

In 1960, the twentieth anniversary of the Battle of Britain prompted the Air Ministry to update its list of eligible squadrons, but No. 53 Squadron remained ineligible. Having made the decision to discriminate between different branches of the air force, it was by then too late fully to make amends, even if there had been the will.

When Bill visited the New Zealand Air Force Museum at Wigram in 1991, he was unaware of these developments and, having seen Jack's name in Westminster Abbey, was surprised that his name was missing from the Battle of Britain Roll of Honour there. Assuming this was an oversight he wrote a polite and dignified letter pointing out the omission:

> *Dear Sir,*
>
> *I recently had the pleasure to visit the Airforce Museum at Wigram. As a war time pilot of 75 Squadron, I would like to express my appreciation and congratulations to all who are responsible for such a wonderful portrayal and memory, not only to those who died in both wars, but to a service which we are all justly proud.*
>
> *May I also express my appreciation to all the volunteers who give their time so fully?*
>
> *On studying the Battle of Britain display and the Roll of Honour of New Zealand airmen, I noted a small omission of my brother's name – Pilot Officer J. C. Mallon, 53 Squadron R.A.F., who died of wounds on 08.10.1940 – shot down in a Blenheim over France. Although his name along with his brother's, P/O T. A. Mallon, is on the Roll of Honour, just recently erected in the Main Hall.*

I am enclosing an extract from the Book of Remembrance displayed in the Battle of Britain Memorial Chapel in Westminster Abbey recording his name. Also proof of the cemetery in which he is buried in France.

I have a full record of the service and photos of His late Majesty King George the 6ᵗʰ at the dedication of the Battle of Britain Chapel, should the Museum wish to take copies.

I trust my letter will be received in the spirit in which it is written and is not meant as a criticism of such a splendid display of the work and dedication of all those responsible.

Yours faithfully,

W. Mallon.

The reply was not what Bill was expecting and he was bitterly disappointed:

Dear Sir,

Thank you for your kind letter and compliments about the R.N.Z.A.F. Museum. It is always nice to get such positive feedback from members of the public, especially those who have been members of the Service.

The Roll of Honour in the Battle of Britain display only lists those men who died while serving with one of the squadrons which qualified them for the Battle of Britain clasp. These were fighter Command Squadrons which included several Blenheim Night Fighter Squadrons. 53 Squadron on the other hand had returned from duties with the B.E.F. in France and was part of Coastal Command at the time of your brother's death. I hope this answers your query.

Yours faithfully,

Therese Angelo

Museum Research Officer

Many years later, with our 'celebrity culture' and obsession with public relations, it may be easier for us to understand the reasons for the War Ministry's decisions and the attitude of the media but, until the day he died, Bill could not understand why men killed in what was essentially the same campaign were treated differently after their deaths.

In 2004, Larry Donnelly D.F.M. wrote a book entitled *The Other Few*, which he described as

> *A long overdue chance to record and celebrate the contribution made by Bomber and Coastal aircrew to the winning of the Battle of Britain.*

In it, he tells the story of these unsung heroes and, in so doing, he does a little to right one of the wrongs in the history of the Battle of Britain. Unfortunately, it came too late for Bill and the memory of his older brother.

A tragic postscript to this story emerged when Barrie Mallon sent me a copy of a letter that had been returned to Jack's sister, May. She had sent it to Jack before his death in 1940 and it had travelled via Australia and South Africa to R.A.F. Detling. Sadly, Jack was killed before the letter arrived and it was returned to May via the unfortunately named 'Dead Letter Office', arriving several months later in 1941.

13 TOM MALLON: 'SAY NOT GOODNIGHT....'

P/O Tom Mallon

'Say not goodnight, but in some brighter clime bid them good morning'

Anna Letitia Barbauld (1743 – 1825)

Details of Tom Mallon's death also emerged after the war, this time from a different source. Tom, like thousands of other volunteers in New Zealand, started his flying career at R.N.Z.A.F. Levin before attending the No. 2 Elementary Flying Training School at Bell Block, the airfield he considered 'home'. He made good progress and, when he left, he felt well-prepared for the next step in his career across the Pacific in Canada.

At RCAF Station Uplands in Ottawa, where he is seen over the page relaxing alongside his North American Harvard, he impressed his instructors so much that after gaining his flying badge he was posted to RCAF Station Mont-Joli, where he worked as a test pilot for over a year. He received a commission and, as Pilot Officer Mallon, was transferred to England, where his proven record as a pilot earned him the opportunity in

May 1944 to serve in No. 488(NZ) Squadron flying the renowned De Havilland Mosquito. The fact that he was flying in a squadron of the R.N.Z.A.F. was a source of great pride to Tom and he was soon participating in operations over enemy territory. Within two weeks, he was actively involved in supporting the invasion forces following the D-Day landings on the 6th June.

Nine months later, while the Mallon crew were fast asleep at R.A.F. Feltwell preparing for a week's Gee-H training, Tom was in the Netherlands preparing for yet another night patrol. At 0420 on the 12th March 1945 Tom and his navigator, P/O George Brock (R.N.Z.A.F.), climbed into their Mosquito Mark XXX (MT484) at Gilze-Rijen airfield.

Tom and George had been together as part of No. 488(NZ) Squadron's night fighter unit since the previous May. They had established themselves as valuable and popular members of the unit, spending their first few months on various bases in the south of England. The squadron was posted to Amiens-Glisy in northern France in November 1944 to support the Allied advance towards Germany and was using Gilze-Rijen in the Netherlands as an advance base.

Their Mosquito took off at 0425 but Tom, despite his vast experience and familiarity with the aircraft, experienced some difficulty handling it on this occasion. Minutes after take-off they crashed into a barn 2.5 km from the runway. Tom and George both suffered serious injuries and died in hospital later that day. Tom had become the second Mallon brother to be killed in action.

Thanks to the generosity of Bill's sons Barrie and Kevin and his sister May's daughter Barbara, I was allowed access to some of the more personal aspects of Tom's death and to experience, however remotely, some of the anguish that Tom's family must have felt when the news of a second family bereavement came through.

On the 14th March 1945, Tom's sister Dora May, known as May to her friends and family, received the telegram that the families of all service personnel dread:

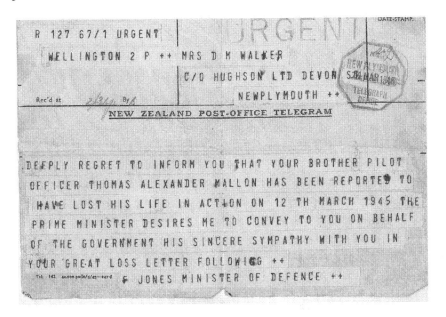

I can only think that May and not her parents received the telegram because she had named herself as Tom's next of kin after Jack's death, to protect her parents if the worse were to happen a second time. Several days later May received a letter from the New Zealand Air Department in Wellington. It gave her more information about the circumstances of Tom's death.

Dear Mrs Walker,

Further to the telegram sent to you by the Hon. the Minister of Defence concerning your brother Pilot Officer Thomas Alexander Mallon I have to advise that the following information has been received from Air Ministry:

Pilot Officer Mallon was a member of the crew of a fighter bomber aircraft which hit trees and a farm-house shortly after take-off at 4.25 a.m. on the 12th March 1945. Pilot Officer Mallon, together with the other member of the crew, lost his life.

On behalf of the Air Board I desire to express my deepest sympathy with you in your great loss, and to assure you that immediately any further information is received you will be advised without delay.

Yours faithfully,

T. A. Barrow. Air Secretary'

P/O. T. A. Mallon, of Bell Block, Taranaki, killed on active service.

In 1949, four years after Tom's death, F/L Leslie Hunt published *'Defence until dawn: the story of 488 (NZ) Squadron'*. In it he recounts in great detail the actions of the squadron's night fighter unit from its formation at Church Fenton, Yorkshire, in June 1942 until it was disbanded in April 1945. At the end of the book, there is the squadron's Roll of Honour, listing all of the squadron's losses, but there are also references throughout the book that provide a far more comprehensive testimony to Tom Mallon and his navigator George Brock.

They are introduced on page 48:

Tom Mallon of Taranaki and George Brock of Palmerston North... were posted in to the squadron and arrived in the early part of May (1944) for their first tour of operations. After a six week stay in Kent the squadron were shipped to Belgium to support the Allied advance but had to spend three weeks afloat because of an 'administrative bungle'. When they eventually arrived at Amiens-Glisy the old French airfield, which had been greatly improved by the Germans, had been badly damaged by sustained Allied bombing.

Tom then gets a special mention on page 72:

Winco Watts and Tom Mallon were responsible for an extraordinary feat of engineering and resourcefulness - the transfer in toto of a 25 foot aircrew hut from one site to another to be later used as the Intelligence 'House of Knowledge.'

And on page 74:

Christmas Eve's 'Peace on Earth' was shattered to some extent when P/O Tom Mallon and F/S George Brock caught up with a Junkers 188 on which they closed and attacked from 300 yards hitting the starboard wing as the Hun returned the compliment with a burst from his upper rear turret. As he peeled off to port Tom fired two further bursts but did not see any strikes and the Junkers disappeared into the haze at 1000 ft. and was not seen again

And their sad, penultimate mention occurs on page 78:

March was again a particularly quiet month with the weather against us and alas was marked by the loss of a fine crew in Tom Mallon and George Brock who crashed when taking off on patrol from our Dutch advance base. (Gilze-Rijen) From the C.O. to the most junior airman came expressions of sorrow at the death of such a grand couple who in a short time had endeared themselves to all and had worked enthusiastically for the squadron. They had given of their best both in the air and on the ground and as the poet says, 'Say not good-night, but in some brighter clime bid them good morning.

Page 94: May 1945:

... A few weeks later, before leaving Holland, the C.O. and I went... to Breda to check that the graves of Tom Mallon and George Brock were being well kept...

The graves of Tom Mallon and George Brock, photographed by the author during a recent trip to Bergen op Zoom in the Netherlands (September 2016)

Tom and George were clearly much loved and respected by their comrades in the squadron.

They were initially buried in Breda, in the Netherlands, 10 km from the crash site, but were later re-interred in the Bergen op Zoom cemetery, 30 km west of Breda.

Much of my blog, and consequently this book, is about the awful tragedies that befell the Mallon family. I found it difficult to grasp the anguish that must have been felt by Alec and Dora, even though I was all too aware that their story had many parallels in other wars, especially the First World War with the slaughter in the trenches of the Somme and the beaches of Gallipoli.

During my research for this book, I came across another New Zealand pilot flying with No. 75(NZ) Squadron, F/O Henry James ('Jim') Murray, who was one of four brothers from Pleasant Point, a small town near Timaru where Jim Haworth was born. His parents were Gordon and Elizabeth Murray and, on the 26th May 1941, one of their sons, David Magnus Murray (27), was killed whilst serving with the New Zealand Infantry in Crete. Just over a year later, on the 22nd July 1942, their eldest son, Gavin Allan Murray (32), a New Zealand Engineer, was killed at El Alamein.

Jim was undeterred, just as Bill and Tom Mallon had been after the loss of their brother Jack, and he continued his pilot training. He was posted to No 75(NZ) Squadron just over a year earlier than Bill, in February 1944, and in the early hours of the 19th April he died, along with three of his crew, when his aircraft was brought down over Denmark on a mine-laying operation in Kiel Bay. He was twenty six and the third of Gordon and Elizabeth's sons to be killed in less than three years.

The Murray brothers are now hundreds of miles apart and, like the Mallons, thousands of miles from home. David has no known grave but his name is engraved on the Athens memorial in Greece, Gavin is buried in the El Alamein cemetery in Egypt and Jim is buried in Gram churchyard in Denmark.

Their surviving brother was not permitted to serve overseas, although both he and their sister did serve with the armed forces in N.Z.

14 TWO SCHOOLS: 'LEST WE FORGET'

Pupils of N.P.B.H.S. standing in front of the school's memorial gate before the war (picture courtesy of the Auckland Museum)

Of course, Jack and Tom Mallon weren't the only former pupils of New Plymouth Boys' High School to lose their lives during the Second World War. When I contacted the school in 2016 to request a copy of the school's Roll of Honour, I was profoundly shocked to discover the number of its old boys killed in the conflict. Given that the period in question was less than six years and the age range of those killed only from about eighteen to forty, I was staggered to learn that the school had lost as many as two hundred and twenty seven young men, sixty two of them serving in the air force, eight of them with No. 75(NZ) Squadron. As Tom Ryder, the head teacher from 1979 to 1995, said in his introduction to the school's Memorial Book 'Lest We Forget':

> *The carnage was great by the measure of any school's war dead. New Plymouth Boys' High School …was recovering from an alarming drop in its boarding roll brought about by the Depression years of the 1930s and … in 1934 the roll was only 490 and yet 227 ex-pupils from this one school, in a small provincial town in New Zealand, died for the causes of*

peace, freedom and democracy in places that span the entire world.

He described the book as:

one man's tribute to his school fellows, some of whom were married with young families, some just getting started in work after years of unemployment and some who had barely dropped their desk-tops for the last time, when they were swept up in war. The biographies range from records of heroic endeavour

A tribute by New Plymouth Boys' High School, New Zealand, to the 227 men of the School who died while serving their Country during the Second World War, 1939-1945.

and sacrifice to brief stories of death by misadventure. They tell of men, some of whom were 'special' as boys, and they tell of many more who were quite unremarkable as boys at school but who were extraordinarily gifted and brave in war. And in every case, whatever the achievement, 'Lest We Forget' tells of men who had a job to do and who got on with it.

The book was produced in 1995 by Jack West, another old boy of the school, and a friend and former boss of Bill Mallon. Its cover, reproduced above, shows the school's stained glass memorial window from its Memorial Hall, with the motto *'Courtesy, courage and wisdom'.*

Jack took on the task of compiling a biography of every one of the two hundred and twenty seven men, from school days to enlistment, from training to action and finally to their deaths. After five years of unremitting research he produced what is an extraordinary tribute.

Thanks to Jack's book and the staff of the school, particularly the senior librarian Stephanie Gibbons, I was able to learn something of the short lives of those killed serving with No. 75(NZ) Squadron. Some of them, like Jack and Tom Mallon, began their love affair with flying at Bell

Block airfield and some even gained their wings at No. 2 Elementary Flying Training School at Bell Block. According to Jack West *'there was probably no aero club in New Zealand with stronger public support than New Plymouth enjoyed ... and there was no finer instructor than Ian Keith at Bell Block'*.

The first of them to die was **Sgt Trevor Hedley Gray**, aged twenty seven. Whilst at school, Trevor had excelled at athletics and gymnastics and later, whilst working for a men's outfitters, had specialised in sprinting and field events with the New Plymouth Athletics Association. He was also a member of the Y.M.C.A. Gymnastic Club's display team for four years and spent a year in the Territorial Army.

He applied to join the R.N.Z.A.F. shortly after the outbreak of war and was awarded his flying badge in March 1941. He left New Zealand for England on the 26th May, waved off by his heavily pregnant wife, Doreen.

Less than two months later, after completing his training on the Wellington bomber, he was posted to R.A.F. Feltwell, the home at that time of No. 75(NZ) Squadron.

The speed with which pilots were being prepared for operational flying at this early stage of the war, in marked contrast to pilots much later in the war like Bill Mallon, was frightening. As second pilot of a Wellington, Trevor had carried out just six operations against targets in Europe when, on the night of 6th November 1941, after being attacked by a German night fighter during a raid on Berlin, his aircraft failed to return. The crew was officially classified as 'missing' and it would be another six years before their families discovered what had happened to their loved ones.

A letter from the Air Department in October 1947 described how their aircraft had crash-landed in marshy land near Akkrum, in the Netherlands:

> *The force of the impact was such that the plane penetrated deeply into the ground and exploded immediately. No bodies were recovered from the crash, nor is it possible to attempt excavation at this stage'.*

The villagers have always believed that the pilot went to great lengths to steer the aircraft away from the village before it crashed and consider the whole crew to be heroes.

Another five years elapsed and in 1952, after the Dutch authorities had decided to salvage the aircraft, the bodies of the six airmen were recovered and buried in the Bergen op Zoom Canadian War Cemetery, close to the cemetery in which Tom Mallon is buried. Trevor left behind his widow, Doreen, and an unseen daughter, Lorraine, who was born the day after her father had sailed from New Zealand.

The German authorities had erected a temporary memorial at the site of the crash, which had long fallen into disrepair, and in 2010 Lorraine became aware of plans by local residents to erect a permanent memorial. She was invited to the unveiling ceremony and, not only did she attend, she was also able to supply information and personal effects that had been returned to her family by the R.A.F. These are now part of a permanent museum display. An image of the memorial, from a photograph by Gebruiker BaykedeVries, appears above.

Four months later, in March 1942, the squadron lost its second N.P.B.H.S. old boy when **P/O Maurice Perrot Bell** was killed, aged

twenty six. Maurice had been a member of both the Stratford Aero Club and the Western Federated Aero Club at Bell Block and qualified as a pilot in April 1941. In October of that year, just two months after his arrival in England, he was posted to the squadron at Feltwell. He started operations almost immediately and continued operational flying for the next five months, surviving a crash landing returning from a raid on Hamburg after just a couple of weeks.

On the 28th March 1942, his Wellington was shot down during an operation to Lubeck in northern Germany. His body was eventually recovered and buried and, on the 3rd April 1950, he was reinterred in the British Military Cemetery in Kiel, Germany.

Later that year, **Sgt Victor Arthur Tunbridge** was killed. Vic was only at N.P.B.H.S. briefly as he had to complete his secondary education at Wellington College when his family relocated. He then worked for the Wellington Woollen Company until he joined the air force in 1941. He was remembered at school as a gifted sportsman and went on to win the Miramar Tennis Club's handicap singles title in Wellington. He also represented Wellington Scottish Harriers in the national cross country championships and won the 'B' Grade provincial title.

He was awarded his wireless operator/air gunner's badge in Canada and was posted to the squadron, by then briefly based at R.A.F. Mildenhall, on the 7th August 1942. On the night of 27th August, after just three weeks and three operations, the Wellington in which Vic was rear gunner failed to return and information received later through the Red Cross confirmed that he had been killed and buried in a cemetery in Körle, near Kassel in Germany. He was reinterred in 1948 in the Hanover War Cemetery. He was twenty eight and left behind his widow, Violet Esther. There was no photograph of Vic in the school's records.

The letter to Bill Mallon from his friend Jack in 1998 had mentioned 1942 being a particularly harrowing year for the squadron, but so too was 1943. Between April and September, four more of the school's old boys lost their lives. The first, **W/O John Arthur Ernest Walsh,** had by far the longest and most varied flying career. He had served for two years in the Territorial Army and applied to join the R.N.Z.A.F. almost immediately after war was declared in September 1939. He was awarded his flying badge in New Zealand on the 22nd Nov 1940 and his first operational posting was to No. 9 Squadron at R.A.F. Honington, in Suffolk, in May 1941. From there he flew

Wellingtons in seven operations over France and Germany.

He was then transferred to the 'Middle East Pool' at Harwell in Berkshire and flew a Wellington to Egypt via Gibraltar and Malta, arriving on the 30th July 1941. In August he was posted to No. 38 Squadron R.A.F. Luqa in Malta and, as Wellington second pilot, he took part in a further nineteen operations to targets in Libya, Sicily and Sardinia. He returned to Egypt in October where, from a landing strip in the Western Desert, he participated in a further seven operations on targets in Libya which completed his first operational tour.

The British Overseas Airways Corporation (Middle East Headquarters) then appealed to Middle East Air Command for the loan of a suitable pilot for about three months to fill a vacancy in one of the crews of their African flights. John was chosen and agreed to the transfer and, in January 1942, he became Second Officer on B.O.A.C. flights from Luxor to Port Sudan and across Equatorial Africa to Kano and Lagos, in Nigeria. In April 1942 he was promoted to Warrant Officer and returned to England by ship from Lagos.

Nine months elapsed before his second operational tour began. On the 10th February 1943, after conversion to the Short Stirling four-engine bomber, he was posted to No 75 (NZ) Squadron, by then at Newmarket in Suffolk. After ten operations his luck finally ran out.

On the 9th April, nine Stirlings took off to join an attack on targets at Duisburg and, on the return flight, a brief distress signal was received from John's aircraft. It was later discovered that it had crashed at Bressingham in Norfolk, thirty four miles short of Newmarket. Soon after impact an explosion was observed and the aircraft burst into flames. It was the first Mk.III Stirling to be lost by the squadron. None of the crew survived and John, who was twenty seven and had married shortly before leaving New Zealand over two years earlier, is buried in Newmarket Cemetery.

Later that month, **Sgt Malcolm Edward John Shogren** was killed. Like Bill Mallon, Malcolm had acquired a good background in engineering at the school and, like Bob, he had become an apprentice on leaving school. He enlisted in September 1941 and, two months later, sailed to Canada where, in June 1942, he was awarded his gunner's badge. He was posted to the squadron at Newmarket in March 1943 and participated in eight operations in a Stirling bomber before disaster struck. His aircraft was one of eight taking part in a mine laying operation in Kiel Bay on the night of 28th April 1943 and one of four that did not return.

Information was received later through the International Red Cross that Malcolm's body had been washed ashore in Denmark, on the 2nd June 1943. He was twenty nine and was buried in Svino churchyard in Denmark. No trace was ever found of the aircraft or the rest of the crew.

F/S Jack Neville Darney, who was twenty two and another gifted sportsman, was the next to lose his life. He had played for both the First XI cricket and the First XV rugby teams at the age of fifteen and, after leaving school in 1936, had worked for New Zealand Railways until he enlisted with the R.N.Z.A.F. in January 1942. He was awarded his 'wings' in September 1942 in Canada, where his rugby prowess blossomed and he was chosen to play on the wing for the Combined Air Forces representative team in a match against the Irish Fusiliers. His play was described by a spectator, also from New Zealand, as *'right up to New Zealand provincial representative standard'.*

He joined the squadron just after it re-located to Mepal in early July 1943, and was killed within three weeks of commencing operational flying.

On the night of the 30th July 1943, on an operation to Remscheid, near Dusseldorf, his Stirling failed to return and it was assumed that the aircraft had been lost at sea. Captured German documents gave no information about the aircraft nor any member of its crew. Together with over twenty thousand other members of Commonwealth Air Forces whose bodies were never recovered, Jack and his crew are remembered at the Runnymede Memorial in Surrey.

F/O Arthur Douglas Howlett was the fourth of the school's old boys with the squadron to die in 1943. The oldest at thirty two, Arthur had arrived in New Zealand as a very young boy when his parents immigrated. After leaving N.P.B.H.S., he worked as a butter maker for the Bell Block Cooperative Dairy Company and enlisted in the summer of 1941. He was awarded his Air Observer's badge in Canada and promoted to Pilot Officer in August 1942.

After a further promotion to Flying Officer, he was posted to the squadron on the 23rd June 1943 and took part in eighteen operations as bomb aimer. On the night of the 23rd September his Stirling bomber was shot down during an operation to Mannheim in south-west Germany.

It was only later confirmed that the bodies of the crew had been recovered and buried in a communal grave, not far from the site of the crash but, in November 1948, Arthur's body was identified and reinterred in an individual grave in Rheinberg Cemetery. Those who remembered Arthur, both from his school-days and during his air force service, spoke of his kindly and considerate nature. Arthur, they said, *'was one of life's gentlemen'.*

The last and youngest of the eight to die was **P/O Ian Edward Blance,** who was twenty one and died in 1944. He had left school in 1937

and, after a spell at New Plymouth Technical College, had found a job at the Mayfair Theatre as a junior projectionist, where he remained until enlisting in February 1942. His half-brother, F/O John William Purcivall D.F.C., also an old boy of the school, was killed in September of that year in a flying accident in Yorkshire.

Ian was awarded his flying badge at Wigram and eventually posted to the squadron in July 1944. He was killed less than three weeks later en route to targets in Stuttgart. On the night of the 28th July, his Lancaster was attacked, probably by one or more Ju-88s, and fatally damaged over France. Struggling with his blazing aircraft, Ian was able to pull the aircraft out of its dive long enough to enable three of his crew to parachute to safety. He and the remaining three crew members crashed to their deaths near the village of Millery.

One crew member was captured by German troops and the other two managed to escape with the help of the Resistance Movement. Ian is buried alongside his three comrades in the Millery Communal Cemetery, close to where they crashed.

Another spin-off from my blog occurred as a result of an e-mail my brother received from Gary Exeter, a Kiwi friend who had worked with him in Nottingham. He had returned to New Zealand over thirty years earlier and was working at **Hereworth School,** an independent Anglican school for boys in Havelock North, Hawke's Bay.

Having read my blog, Gary had asked a colleague with an interest in the school's history if he knew of any old boys who had served with No. 75(NZ) Squadron. All he could locate was a list of those killed in the war, but using this and the squadron's roll of honour I was able to identify the relevant airmen and complete a small part of the school's proud history.

P/O William Willis (33), a pilot, was killed on the 22nd May 1944 when his Lancaster was shot down during a raid on Duisburg. William, pictured below on the left, is commemorated at the Runnymede Memorial in Surrey.

F/S John Gilbertson (22), right in this picture, was also a pilot. He took off from R.A.F. Feltwell in Wellington BJ661 at about 2300 on the 28th July 1942 bound for Hamburg. The crew had completed their bombing run and were over the IJsselmeer (Lake IJssel) in the Netherlands on their

homeward journey when, at 0305, they were attacked from beneath by a German night fighter, a Messerschmitt Bf110, piloted by Oberstleutnant Wolfgang Kuthe. Their aircraft crashed into the water and broke in two, allowing two of the five man crew to escape. Sergeants Ron Callaghan (left) and Alan Rutherford, both R.N.Z.A.F., were picked up and are seen in the top photograph being helped from a German rescue launch. They were eventually incarcerated in P.O.W. camp Stalag VIIIB in Poland.

The aircraft was hoisted out of the water within hours of the crash (see lower photograph), apparently so that the Germans could learn as much as possible about the aircraft's navigation system. The bodies of John Gilbertson and his navigator, F/S Martin Byrne (R.N.Z.A.F.), were discovered, still strapped in their seats. Both are buried in Amsterdam's New Eastern Cemetery. Both of these photographs are courtesy of Michel Beckers.

Gunner Sgt William Titcomb (R.A.F.V.R.) was thrown from the aircraft in the crash and his body, washed up several days later, was interred in the Harderwijk Cemetery on the shore of the IJsselmeer. All three of the deceased were buried by the Germans with full military honours.

F/S Lloyd Chamberlain (28), an air gunner, was killed on the 12th March 1942 when his Wellington was lost without trace on an operation to Emden. Pictured on the right below, he is commemorated at the Runnymede Memorial.

Sgt Patrick Hunter (29), on the left, was a navigator. He was killed on the 28th April 1943 when his Stirling was lost without trace during a mine-laying operation in Heligoland, one of twenty  two aircraft lost that night. He also is commemorated at the Runnymede Memorial.

F/S Ian Smith (34), a bomb aimer, was killed on the 1st September 1943 during an attack on targets in Berlin. This was a bad night for Bomber Command, with eighteen bombers lost, including four Stirlings from No.75 (NZ) Squadron. F/S Smith is buried in the Rheinberg War Cemetery in Germany. Unfortunately, I was unable to locate a picture of Ian.

S/L Wilfred Williams D.F.C. (31) was the C.O. of No. 1 O.T.U. in New Zealand, where he had returned in 1942 after service as a pilot stretching back to 1935, including a spell with No.311 (Czechoslovak) Squadron as well as No.75 (NZ) Squadron. He was killed in an accident shortly after take-off in a Lockheed Hudson Mk.VI at Ohakea on the 15th July 1943. He left behind a wife and young son, as well as an unborn son.

In June 2015 Chris Newey e-mailed me with some more information about Wilfred, pictured here in 1940:

> *Wilfred Williams was a foundation member of No. 75(NZ) Squadron, and in fact was one of the pilots assembled in the U.K. in 1937 to form the No. 1 New Zealand Flight to fly the N.Z. government's thirty newly-purchased Wellington bombers to New Zealand. When the war broke out the New Zealand government gave the Wellingtons back to Britain and it was agreed that a New Zealand heavy bomber squadron would be formed in the R.A.F. with the N.Z. personnel remaining to participate in the conflict.*

It would be wrong to think that there was anything unusual about the enormous losses suffered by these two schools. Christchurch Boys' High School, for example, Jim Haworth's old school, lost over two hundred former students during WW2, eleven of them serving with No. 75(NZ) Squadron., and this story was repeated across New Zealand.

A common thread in the stories of many of these airmen, apart from the enormous depth of talent they possessed, is the time they spent training in Canada. In July 2016, the newsletter of the New Zealand Bomber Command Association featured the reminiscences of Ron Mayhill D.F.C., a bomb aimer with the squadron during the summer of 1944. Ron is president of the association and also the author of *'Bombs on target'*, a graphic account of his time with the squadron from June 1944 until he was wounded during an operation over France on the 31st August 1944.

> *We old fellows are surely allowed a little reminiscing, something not to be confused with dwelling in the past.*
>
> *We were young, a fierce war was raging and we volunteered for aircrew.*
>
> *We wore our uniforms proudly, a white flash in our caps at I.T.W., we passed all our tests and were found sound in body, mind and nerve.*

We were called the 'cream of youth' by some and 'Blue Orchids' by others not as privileged.

Most of us became part of the British Commonwealth Air Training Plan (B.C.A.T.P.) that promised the dream of flying and going overseas, and all of it free. Not all would become Pilots and most trained as Observer/Navigators or Wireless Operator/Air Gunners.

The B.C.A.T.P. was a vast scheme in a vast country with training stations spread across 5,000 km from British Columbia to Prince Edward Island. At its peak 3,000 a month gained their wings.

How exciting it was for a great bunch of keen, impressionable young men to experience different culture, customs, speech, food and pastimes. We withstood extremes of temperature, from scorching hot to 50 degrees below. We enjoyed a great variety of sights, from mighty Rockies to seemingly endless, featureless Prairies, enormous Great Lakes, spectacular Leaf Fall, Niagara Falls and an unforgettable embarkation leave in New York.

We have so many happy memories and photos of Canada. The friendly people opened their homes to us on our leaves and some (of us) even brought brides back home.

It was an experience of a lifetime for the 7,000 New Zealanders who trained in Canada, a remarkable preparation for the realities and uncertainties of war that lay ahead.

15 NAVIGATION: 'WHAT THE EYE DOESN'T SEE…..'

A Lancaster navigator at work. This is F/O Phil Ingleby, who was killed on the 7th August 1944 during bombing exercises on the Lincolnshire coast (picture courtesy of I.W.M.)

As the navigator of a heavy bomber, the challenges Jim faced were enormous, particularly in the rapidly changing circumstances of an operation at night. The role of navigator has been described as the 'most cerebral' of all the roles in an aircraft, and this was certainly the case in the days before they were fitted with the most up-to-date equipment. The importance of the role is emphasised in this letter from the C.O. of Santa Ana Army Air Base in the U.S., sent in 1944 to the parents of a recruit, disappointed not to have been selected for pilot training (from *The Wild Blue*' by Stephen Ambrose):

> *Your son has been selected by the Classification Board for training as a navigator. I congratulate both you and him on this achievement. The position of navigator is one of utmost importance in the combat team. The pilot and bombardier are dependent upon his skill and speed in making*

necessary calculations to insure the success of the mission

Throughout the war, work was going on to improve navigation technology, primarily to improve the accuracy of bombing, and no-one played a more significant role in these developments than Alan Dower Blumlein. Blumlein, an English electronics engineer credited with inventing the recording and playback of stereo sound, was honoured in April 2015 for his pioneering work in that field at a special ceremony held at E.M.I.'s Abbey Road Studios in London. What is probably more significant, and less well known, is the role he played in the development of H2S airborne radar, a system widely credited as a factor in shortening the Second World War.

Alan died on the 7th June 1942, aged 38, during a secret trial of H2S when the Halifax bomber in which he was flying crashed at Welsh Bicknor in Herefordshire. Blumlein's role in the project was a closely guarded secret at the time and consequently only a brief announcement of his death was made some two years later, to avoid giving comfort to the enemy.

After the Battle of Britain, R.A.F. Bomber Command had begun night attacks against German cities. Navigation in the dark was very difficult, particularly if there was cloud cover over the ground, and at first

Alan Dower Blumlein (1903 – 1942)
(picture: E.M.I. Group Archive Trust)

crews had to rely on dead reckoning, which involved estimating position by speed, flying time and compass readings. Unpredictable winds could disrupt the finest calculations.

Although the R.A.F. had initially reported good results from the raids, an independent analysis in 1941 based on daylight air reconnaissance showed that half the bombs fell on open country and only one bomb in ten hit the target - and the report counted a 'hit' if the bomb fell within five miles of the target! In the crucial Ruhr Valley, the centre of German

industrial production, only one in fifteen was on target and all this failure
had been at the cost of about 700 British bombers.

Raids on Germany were more or less suspended until 1942 when
the 'Area bombing' strategy was introduced and radio electronics promised
some improvement in targeting. A radio navigation system called 'Gee' was
developed and introduced from about March 1942, as well as another
medium-range navigation scheme known as 'Oboe', which was mostly used
on De Haviland Mosquitos and was able to guide single aircraft more
accurately to the target. Towards the end of 1943, Gee was refined as Gee-
H using an aircraft mounted transmitter in conjunction with those on the
ground. All of these systems were dependent on radio transmitters in
England and were limited in range.

H2S, the first airborne ground-scanning radar system, performed
its first experimental flight on the 23rd April 1942 with the radar mounted
in a Halifax bomber. It was designed to identify targets on the ground for
night and all-weather bombing and its first operational use was on the 30th
January 1943, when thirteen 'Pathfinder' bombers set out to mark targets in
Hamburg. It was initially fitted to Stirling and Halifax bombers, mounted in
a 'radome', but in the summer of 1943 the R.A.F. began to equip Lancasters
with this new navigation aid.

H2S was vital in the air battle for Berlin, a series of large raids on
the German capital and other cities from November 1943 until March 1944,
as Berlin was out of range of Gee and Oboe and often obscured by cloud in
the winter. The H2S sets available at the start of the battle were not
particularly effective and it was not until December 1944, when the H2S
Mark III was successfully used for the first time, that it became possible to
bomb Berlin accurately. The Mark III could clearly identify open and built-
up spaces beneath the aircraft.

A modification of H2S, called 'Fishpond', also used a radar scanner
in the aircraft to identify enemy aircraft to a range of up to thirty miles. H2S
had a surprisingly long lifetime, equipping almost all Bomber Command
aircraft during the late war period and beyond. An advanced version, the
Mk. 9, was developed for the post-war V bomber fleet and H2S was last
used in anger during the Falklands War in 1982 on the Avro Vulcan. Some
units remained in service on the Handley Page Victor aircraft until 1993.

The picture of AA-W flown by Bill Mallon (below) during No. 75(NZ) Squadron's last war operation shows an H2S radome, with clear perspex aft, fitted below the fuselage.

Nearly sixty years later, in his interview in 2004, Bill demonstrated that he still had a pretty good grasp of how it all worked:

We had H2S, we had Gee and then we had what they called GeeH.......They all came along in progress as they were invented or progressed so they were fitted to the various stations. H2S was a scanner which took a photo of the ground and from that the navigator could use navigation points on the ground to recognise if we are on course or off course and would make adjustments accordingly. And the same with the Gee which was a radar mechanism which gave coordinates in which he used again to retain you on course.

When asked about bombing when the target was covered in cloud

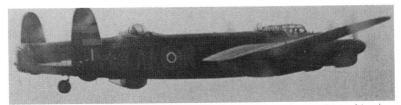

Lancaster AA-W with H2S radome below (picture: E. Ware, NZBCA Archives)

Bill described the role of the Pathfinder squadrons in ensuring the accuracy of the bombing:

They dropped the target indicators greens, reds, yellows and such like which lit up on the clouds and you bombed on those. When they had master bombers, which was when I was operational, the master bomber would call you on VHF (we had VHF as well as ordinary HF radio in the aircraft) and he might tell you to change the aiming point. He would have it re-marked by the pathfinders and then tell the main force that they should now bomb on greens - that's how he controlled the raid.

Anyone who reads Jim Haworth's letters cannot help but be struck by his wicked sense of humour and this is as true when describing his experiences navigating an aircraft as it is when writing about senior officers in the air force or the progress of the war. After one particularly harrowing operation in which three aircraft were shot down Jim wrote:

Funny to think of it, but I haven't seen a bit of flak yet myself. I believe in what the eye doesn't see, the less pants are dirtied, so just keep the old head behind the curtain in my part of the dog-box.

During the winter of 1943-44, under the British Commonwealth Air Training Plan (B.C.A.T.P.), Jim had found himself posted for training as a navigator to No. 5 A.O.S. (Air Observers' School) in Winnipeg, in the province of Manitoba, Canada. Fairly soon after arriving, he was flying as 'Second Navigator' on an Avro Anson without any of the new navigation aids on board. Here are his observations, written to his wife during a cold, dark evening of a Canadian winter on the 13th February 1944.

Started to snow this morning and is quite warmish to what we have had. We flew one day last week with a temperature of -26°C up at six thousand feet and believe me after the first half hour we really froze. I did mentally anyhow and being only 2nd Navigator that day had a loaf after that. Poking your head out of a side window to check courses on the sun with the astro compass and taking shots out of the top hatch is no joke in that temperature. So after one or two attempts just called it a day. When you are a 2nd Nav you only have a collapsible (literally) seat to sit on and a collapsible table to work on and usually the 1st Nav is trying to get past to get a pin point or so from behind the bomb aimer's seat, which is alongside the pilot and just in front of this d--- table. So usually you sit on the spare parachute in the rear of the wireless operator, and try to balance log and 2 books of air tables in each hand while working out each sextant shot. If it is at night you also have to use a torch to see what you are trying to read or do. So summing up everything it's just 'loovely' being 2nd Nav. In between times you are trying to thaw your fingers out so you can write at all.

You might just be interested in the routine of checking the course at night on a star – without a torch as it was one night! First step (of umpteen to and fro) – you fit the little thingymybob (the astro compass(sometimes called numerous other things)) in the appropriate mount and then find that you have omitted to remember the star is now on the port side, not starboard, so you fumble in the dark and undo the little clamp holding it, after once more taking off one glove which you have replaced after taking it off to fix the darned thing – then you once more get it clamped into the correct mount (there is one for each side) and open the side window and push the outfit into the fitting. Then seeing it's dark and you have no torch you try and see the levels to level it up with thumb screws fore and aft and otherwise, but you can't see them so you do it by guess and by God. Next you have to check the compass itself on a known bearing on a wing tip (no time to do this before you left) as they are usually out a few degrees.

Then – at last you can start to do what you started out to do – take a bearing on the star selected. So you turn the little knob and get the little chappie (the star) all lined up but – blast it! – you can't see what time your watch reads – so you dash up to the W.A.G and by the light of his little light get a dim view of your ticker and keeping that in your noodle as your pad seems to have done a bunk in the black-out, you next dash back, pull the astro compass out of the mount and dash back to the little light to read the bearing then – whew! About halfway now – close the window in case the W.A.G does his block as he is just ahead of it –then you put up your little collapsible seat and table again – which the 1st Nav between times has put down - and get out your 2 books of words – pardon – tables, and go to work on working out what the course is or rather what the tables say it is.

By that time the 1st Nav has asked you about half a dozen times if you have got 'it', 'it' being the correct course, and at last has given up the ghost and taken the magnetic compass as read and plotted this in.

By now you are wondering what all this is for – well, you see, the little compasses they install usually have a small error which has been recorded for the unwary, but somehow or other this doesn't always stay put so it is necessary to do all this work to check it.

Finally by this time the 1st Nav has altered course and you do the whole proceeding again.

How do you like it? Of course when you have a torch or in the daytime it is not quite so complicated and I have managed to do it in about two and a half minutes. In fact the other day we had an evasive action exercise, 2 series of about 6 alterations of courses with only 5 minutes between. Believe me I was a busy man that day.

I'm sure that Sally must have taken some comfort from the tone of his letters, even though she would have been worried sick that something terrible could happen at any time.

Ruth found a poem in her dad's hand writing recently, written on the back of a piece of flight chart that had been torn off. She doesn't know for sure, but she believes it to be her dad's handiwork and, from what I have learned about Jim during the last four years, I would have to agree. It was definitely written by one of the squadron's navigators. There is a glossary below for those unfamiliar with R.A.F. slang and the range of techniques at the navigator's disposal, long before global positioning satellites were available.

To the Tune of "The Mountains of Mourne" (A burn mark made identification of the title very difficult!)

At Mepal our briefing's a wonderful sight

The Sprog navigators all shitting with fright

They don't hold with loops or use astro at all

Their only way home is a bloody Gee crawl

At least from their logs it would so appear

That they just guess a course for the skipper to steer

With D.R.M. setting and blue end in red

It's no wonder they're always so late into bed.

When all's said and done they must know their stuff

When the vis. has clamped down & the Met is all duff

With H2S fixes and DR as well

And API winking like a bat out of hell

And revise ETA they just alter course

And hope to be still with the rest of the force

But when 'H' hour comes round & TI's go down

You can bet Seventy-five will be raining bombs down.

When coming back home with the crew all asleep

The Nav working backward to fill in his gaps

Across the North Sea they erratically roam

Believing the Nav when he says 'Soon be home'.

And when at long last the poor bastards arrive

A sweet voice from control says turn '25'.

Glossary

Astro	Astronavigation – using celestial bodies and a sextant to fix the aircraft's position
A.P.I.	Air Position Indicator
D.R.	Dead Reckoning - calculating one's current position by using a previously determined position and estimated speed over an elapsed time.
D.R.M.	Direct Reading Magnetic compass. Blue end in red probably refers to the N. and S. poles of the compass, coloured red and blue respectively.
E.T.A.	Estimated time of arrival
Gee	An early form of ground control radar
H2S	Aircraft mounted radar
H Hour	The moment bombs are scheduled to start to fall
Loops	Loop antennae, part of the Radio Direction Finder system (R.D.I.)

Met	The Meteorology Officer's weather report
Sprog	A newly qualified airman
T.I.s	Target Indicator flares dropped by Pathfinder Force
Vis	Visibility

The map below shows the distances that Jim had to navigate. Mepal to Gelsenkirchen was a relatively short trip of four hundred miles each way, or just under five hours, whereas Mepal to Potsdam was a massive seven hundred miles each way, a trip lasting eight and a half hours.

Some bombers even attacked Milan, in northern Italy, earlier in the war, a distance of over eight hundred miles each way! The distances covered were in fact much greater as, to make life more difficult for the enemy's defences, bombers never flew a direct route to their target.

Hundreds of aircraft were lost during the war as a result of

A hand-drawn map showing all eight of the crew's war operations, as well as Bob's extra operation to Merseburg with the Taylor crew

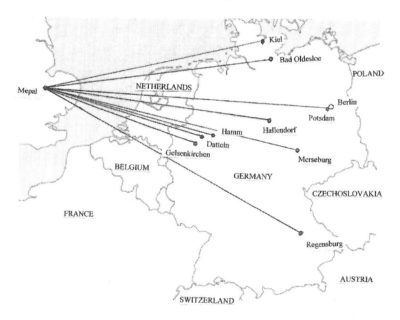

navigational errors, especially during the early years. Given the relatively primitive methods of navigation and the inaccuracy of the meteorological information, it is testimony to the skill of the navigators that this number was not considerably higher. I have nothing but the greatest admiration for these men, often operating in the most challenging of conditions.

16 THREE LANCASTERS: JANE, VERA AND WILLIE

NX611, LE-C/DX-C ('Just Jane')

NX611, 4th April 2012, East Kirkby, Lincolnshire

During the four years I have been researching my dad's story, three Avro Lancasters have taken on particular significance. The first is **NX611**, whose majestic presence was the highlight of our regular trips to Lincoln as it and its predecessor, R5868, stood as 'gate guardians' at R.A.F. Scampton more or less constantly from 1960 to 1983.

NX611 was built at the Austin factory in Longbridge in April 1945, one of the first Mk VII Avro Lancasters destined to be part of the R.A.F.'s 'Tiger Force'. It soon became surplus to requirements and was placed in storage until 1952. There followed a spell as part of the French government's Naval Air Arm, then air sea rescue and cartography duties before flying to Sydney for an overhaul by the Historical Aircraft Preservation Society. The 12,000 mile flight back to Biggin Hill in Britain in 1965 took seventy flying hours over nine days.

Meanwhile, in Lincolnshire, brothers Fred and Harold Panton were determined to commemorate the death of their brother Christopher, who was killed on the infamous Nuremburg Raid of March 1944, as well as all of the others killed whilst serving in Bomber Command. When some land came up for sale which included part of the defunct East Kirkby airfield, they bought it and began to renovate the working area of the airfield. They built a new hangar where an original T2 hangar had stood and started to look for a Second World War Bomber.

When NX611 came up for auction in 1972, the brothers thought it would be the perfect monument but the reserve price was not met and the aircraft was sold privately, eventually replacing R5868 at Scampton. Undeterred, the brothers kept up their efforts and eventually a deal was struck. In September 1983, they finally purchased it and, after completing the agreed total of ten years at R.A.F. Scampton, she was brought to East Kirkby. After a complete and on-going overhaul, 'Just Jane' as she is now known is giving displays and taxi runs for the public.

On the 4th April 2012, sixty seven years to the day after my dad's operation to Merseburg with the Taylor crew, I was able to fulfil a childhood dream and stand in my dad's position in the cockpit of a Lancaster, as one by one its four Merlin engines roared into life. It was raining so heavily that water ran down the inside of the perspex, dripped onto my neck and shoulders and trickled over the Flight Engineer's panel. Compared to the conditions endured by crews on an operation, though, this was comfort - I was only going to taxi a couple of hundred yards, not fly 1,200 miles at twenty thousand feet over enemy territory for eight hours.

It is difficult to describe the emotions I felt as this impressive aircraft slowly rolled across what is left of the airfield. I couldn't help but think of my dad, doing exactly the same thing all those years ago, but the fifty five thousand

Looking over the pilot's shoulder in NX611, April 2012

Allied airmen for whom this experience would be their last on British soil were also in my thoughts.

My dad would have been the first to remind me to spare a thought also for the half million or so civilians killed by the Allied bombing campaign, not to mention the sixty million victims of the war across the rest of the world. For those few minutes, I felt closer to my dad than I had for nearly forty years.

FM213, VR-A (Vera)

A view from the flight engineer's position in VR-A, 18th August 2014

Just under two years later, in February 2014, my sister sent me a link to a newspaper article about the Canadian Warplane Heritage Museum's plans to fly their Lancaster to England in August for a month-long visit. Members of the public were invited to pay an enormous amount of money for the privilege of taking a thirty minute flight. When would such an opportunity come again? Within twenty four hours I had joined the C.W.H.M. on line and booked a flight. It would take place on the 18th August 2014 at Humberside Airport, formerly R.A.F. Kirmington.

The aircraft, a Mark X originally designated FM213, was built at the Victory Aircraft factory in Malton, Ontario, in 1945. It was subsequently re-designated **KB726 VR-A**, the 'Mynarski Memorial Lancaster', in memory of Pilot Officer Andrew Mynarski, a Canadian air gunner posthumously awarded the Victoria Cross.

P/O Mynarski had died exactly a week after D Day, when his aircraft was attacked by a Ju88 during an operation over northern France. He had tried desperately to help free the rear gunner, P/O Pat Brophy, who was trapped in his turret as their aircraft was engulfed in flames. Andrew eventually bailed out, badly burned and with a fire-damaged parachute, but died later in a German field hospital. Miraculously, the rest of the crew survived, including the rear gunner who was thrown clear when the aircraft crashed.

After a number of delays VR-A, or Vera as she is known, left Hamilton, Ontario on the 4th August. Pacifying a restless crowd of well-wishers in Hamilton, who were frustrated by the delays in her departure, pilot David Rohrer shared a classic piece of advice given to him when he was a keen and impatient trainee: *'It's always better to be down here wishing you were up there, than to be up there wishing you were down here.'* I can imagine my dad and thousands of other airmen saying 'hear, hear!' to that.

She arrived at a wet and windy R.A.F. Coningsby in Lincolnshire on the 8th August, following stops at Goose Bay in Labrador, Canada, Narsarsuaq in Greenland and Keflavik in Iceland. Shortly after arriving, she underwent a scheduled maintenance inspection and then the Canadian crews completed a short training program in preparation for air displays and fly pasts with the only other air-worthy Lancaster in the world, PA474, the Battle of Britain Memorial Lancaster - and a week of flights for a small number of lucky paying customers.

Humberside Airport on Monday the 18th August 2014 was a real family affair. One of my daughters and her flying enthusiast husband had arrived from Cambridgeshire with their two year-old son, who for months afterwards thought his granddad was on every plane that flew over their house. My wife and our granddaughter had accompanied me from North Yorkshire and my sister and her partner had travelled the short distance from Cleethorpes, together with her two grandsons who were over from Cheshire.

Then my brother and his wife arrived from their home in Nottingham with a huge surprise. In a carrier bag and wrapped in tissue paper was the jumper that my dad had worn throughout his time with No. 75 (NZ) Squadron. I just had to try it on and wondered if I should wear it on the flight. When the pilot discovered its provenance he said he wouldn't allow me on the aircraft unless I was wearing it!

Standing alongside 'VeRA' – in that jumper

I have to admit I found it difficult to speak for a few minutes after pulling it on but we were soon whisked away for our briefing and five excited passengers were given instructions on how to evacuate the aircraft if the worst were to happen. We didn't anticipate any problems, unlike Bob who feared the worst every time he climbed aboard, all those years ago.

At last it was time to take the short mini-bus journey to 'VeRA' waiting on the tarmac. We boarded and buckled up in the seats bolted in place on the port side of the fuselage, just behind the main spar. The first time I had been in a Lancaster two years earlier, heard the roar of the engines and felt it start to move had been an emotional experience, but this was on another level entirely.

As we taxied towards the runway my nervous excitement couldn't hide an overwhelming feeling of sadness - because I was unable to share this with my dad, because he had missed so much since his premature death and because of the thousands of young men who had died shortly after boarding an aircraft and going through an experience just like this.

We taxied to the end of the runway and turned. After just a few seconds waiting the noise level started to increase dramatically and we started to accelerate. Like my dad, by this stage my emotions were beginning to subside as practical considerations took over. I started to visualise the actions of the pilot and the flight engineer as we gained speed and the noise level continued to rise. I pictured the pilot pushing the throttles forward evenly with his right hand whilst he controlled the inevitable swing to the left with careful use of the rudders.

As we passed the airport terminal the flight engineer would be taking over control of the throttles with his left hand as the pilot pushed the control column forward with both hands to raise the tail and achieve take-off attitude. As the speed crept up to 90 knots, just 103 m.p.h., he would start pulling back on the control column taking the aircraft into a shallow climb, so shallow that I was not even aware that we had left the ground until I looked down and saw the runway receding below.

Compared to taking off in a modern passenger jet this was like a drive in an old and very noisy bus, a feeling that added to the disbelief that we were really airborne. Shortly after take-off the flight engineer raised the undercarriage, we banked to the right and we were given permission to unfasten our seat belts.

We soon reached our cruising speed of about a hundred and fifty knots and continued at an altitude of between five hundred and a thousand feet. The views were stunning, something I doubt Bob would have had much time to appreciate over the fields of Cambridgeshire as he filled in the Flight Engineer's log. Interestingly, our Flight Engineer spent most of his time monitoring gauges and filling in his log, too.

I had lived most of my life in this part of Lincolnshire, so as well as soaking up the experience I was able to identify most of the landmarks and a few of the Bomber Command bases the pilot included in his thirty minute flight, including:

R.A.F. Kirmington, our starting point, home at various stages of the war to **Nos. 150, 166 and 153 Squadrons** which between them lost a total of 178 bombers, 127 Lancasters and 51 Wellingtons.

R.A.F. North Killingholme, home from January 1944 to **No. 550 Squadron** which lost 62 of its Lancasters.

R.A.F. Grimsby, formerly Waltham aerodrome, home to **No. 142** and then **No. 100 Squadron** which lost 48 Wellingtons and 116 Lancasters respectively.

After a few minutes, any attempt to identify the rest of the airfields, much less photograph them, was almost impossible. I had to deal with my

Holton le Clay. The 'Jug and Bottle' pub, at the bottom of the picture, was built on the site of one of the dispersal points of R.A.F. Grimsby (Waltham)

emotions, the wish to view the aircraft from different positions and savour the whole experience, as well as a mild feeling of nausea that had started to creep over me. I have never been the best of travellers but, at 150 knots on a windy day in August, there was more movement than I was comfortable with. I eventually found the position which gave me the most relief, standing on my seat with my head and shoulders in the mid-upper gun turret, where I had an amazing view in all directions and plenty of fresh air.

All too soon, the flight came to an end and the aircraft touched down effortlessly on the tarmac. Despite my mixed emotions during my thirty minutes in the air, I had felt none of the nervousness that I usually experience when flying, testimony to my faith in this incredible aircraft. It wasn't the most comfortable of trips, but I wouldn't have missed it for the world.

At 6.45 p.m. on Saturday the 14th of April 1945 the Mallon crew had taken off from Mepal on the longest of their operations en route to targets at Potsdam on the outskirts of Berlin. They didn't touch down until 3.14 the following morning., eight and a half hours later. Memorable as my flight was, the thought of an eight and a half hour round trip to Berlin, not knowing if you would return, was almost impossible to imagine.

As we taxied towards the airport building, my thoughts returned once again to those young men, seventy years earlier. Their immense relief at returning from a flight into Hell would have been diminished by the knowledge that they would have to do it all again, possibly the next day, and keep on doing it until their tour was complete or the worst really did happen. My dad, along with every other war veteran I have ever listened to, said he wasn't brave, just terrified. He wasn't a fan of John Wayne either, but I'm sure he would have appreciated the actor's description of courage: *'Courage is being scared to death ...... and saddling up anyway.'*

Other airfields close to our flight path, with squadrons and losses, were:

Kelstern - No. 625 Squadron, lost 70 Lancasters

Strubby - No. 619 Squadron, lost 65 Lancasters

Spilsby - Nos. 207 and **44 Squadrons**, total losses, 85 Lancasters.

East Kirkby - Nos. 57 and **630 Squadrons**, total losses, 121 Lancasters in operations and another 29 in crashes and accidents.

Coningsby - Nos. 106, 97, 619, 61 and **83 Squadrons** and, for six months from August 1943, **No. 617 Squadron**, the 'Dam busters'. Total losses, 101 Lancasters, 57 Hampdens and 17 Manchesters

Woodhall Spa - Nos. 106, 97 and **619 Squadrons. No. 617 Squadron** carried out its famous 'Tirpitz' raid after being transferred to Woodhall Spa in January 1945, and Guy Gibson, its former leader, was killed flying a Mosquito on an operation with **No. 627 Squadron**, based here from April 1944 to September 1945. Total losses, 74 Lancasters and 17 Mosquitoes.

Bardney - No. 9 Squadron, lost 85 Lancasters

Fiskerton - Nos. 49, 576 and **550 Squadrons**, total losses, 117 Lancasters

Dunholme Lodge - Nos. 44 and **619 Squadrons**, total

losses, 120 Lancasters

Wickenby - **Nos. 12** and **626 Squadrons**, total losses, 190 Lancasters and 6 Wellingtons

Faldingworth - **No. 300 Squadron** (mainly Polish aircrews), lost 37 Lancasters

Hemswell - **Nos. 61** and **144 Squadrons** and later **Nos. 150** and **170 Squadrons**. Total losses, 83 Hampdens, 62 Wellingtons, 1 Manchester and 22 Lancasters

Blyton - **No. 199 Squadron**, lost 1 Wellington and 50 Lancasters

Bottesford - **Nos. 207** and **467** (mainly Australian-manned) **Squadrons** and in 1944 for the D-Day landings the USAAF. Total RAF losses, 3 Manchesters and 55 Lancasters

Elsham Wolds -**Nos. 103, 576** and **100 Squadrons**, total losses, 208 Lancasters, 28 Wellingtons and 12 Halifaxes.

The scale of these losses, a total of 3,491 aircraft lost from all Lincolnshire airfields, is horrific but obscures the terrible loss of life that lost aircraft represent. Of the 55,573 Bomber Command aircrew that lost their lives, 25,611 had flown from Lincolnshire and adjacent airfields. The story is repeated across all counties on the east of the country with the airfields in Cambridgeshire, a much smaller county and home to R.A.F. Mepal, losing more than 1,400 aircraft and over 10,000 airmen.

RF127, AA-W ('Willie')

Towards the end of the war, when the Mallon crew was at Mepal, the squadron was so over-manned that it was unlikely that any crew could legitimately claim 'ownership' of a particular aircraft. Bob's nine operations were completed in five different aircraft and during his four months of flying with the squadron he flew in nine altogether.

Despite this, being able to claim one particular aircraft as your own must have provided a degree of comfort for many and, in a letter to his wife on the 25th April 1945, Jim had written enthusiastically about what he believed was to be the crew's new aircraft.. *'Did I mention we have a new kite,*

W for Willie? Quite a newish job with all the latest bits and pieces in it.....' It was several months later before I realised the significance of that particular aircraft.

Trawling through old photographs of Lancasters was always a thrill if I discovered one with the identifying letters AA or JN, signifying that it belonged to No. 75(NZ) Squadron, and on a few occasions the dates confirmed that the aircraft in question was at Mepal when my dad was there. On a couple of occasions I even found pictures of aircraft that my dad had flown in. Imagine my excitement when I discovered a grainy photograph taken on the 24th April 1945 during the squadron's final war

AA-W (RF127) en route to Bad Oldesloe, 24th April 1945 (picture: E. Ware, NZBCA Archives)

operation, a daylight raid on Bad Oldesloe in northern Germany.

The aircraft closest to the camera is clearly **AA-W**, or 'W Willie' as Jim and others called it, which at that stage of the war was **RF127**. The O.R.B. and the crews' log books confirm that it is the aircraft in which the Mallon crew was flying on that day. The heads visible in the cockpit are those of Bob and Bill and Don Cook, the twenty year old mid-upper gunner, can be seen even more clearly in his turret. This picture of my dad in the air force may not be the clearest I have seen, but I treasure it far more than the formal pictures of him in his 'Best Blues'.

17 'CLOSING THE FAMILY CIRCLE'

L to R: second cousins Barrie Mallon, Patricia Colley and Kevin Mallon, April 2015

As the 2015 centenary of Anzac day approached, Patricia Colley was busy at home in New South Wales, Australia, knitting poppies for the Bathurst R.S.L. (Returned and Services League of Australia). These were to be placed on crosses to mark the local war dead and whilst engaged in this task Patricia was thinking about the family she had in New Zealand but had never met and the possibility of making contact.

Patricia's grandmother was May Elizabeth Mallon, the sister of Alec Mallon, Bill's father, who had emigrated to New Zealand in 1910 after returning from service in the Boer War. She remembered vividly as a small child in the late 1920s waving off her grandparents as they sailed from Sydney to visit 'Uncle Alec', who by that time had married and had four children, Tom, Jack and twins Bill and Dora May.

The families lost touch and in 2015 all Patricia could recall was that Uncle Alec and Aunty Dora had lived in Taranaki and had twins. She also remembered her grandmother showing her a 1940 newspaper clipping reporting Jack Mallon missing in action, the same picture I had published in my blog. She knew nothing of the full extent of the tragedy that had befallen the family.

Patricia's son-in-law, Michael Knight, agreed to research the family using this limited information and very soon came across my blog. He was fascinated to read the story of the Mallon family and Patricia read with amazement about the family's tragic losses. On the 28th January 2015, I received an e-mail from Michael:

Hi Vic,

I am emailing firstly to thank you for your wonderful blog containing details of the Mallons. My wife's mother (Patricia Colley), here in Australia, is related to them as her grandmother May Elizabeth Mallon and Alexander Mallon were brother and sister. Pat has lost contact with the Mallons many many years ago with only a sketchy recollection of Alexander and some of the family visiting his sister May in Sydney. Pat knew the sons were pilots but very little of the details. I printed out a number of the chapters and pictures from your blog which she read with pride. Thank you for publishing it.

My second reason for emailing is to attempt to establish contact with the remaining Mallons in New Zealand. From your blog I have been able to discover the names of some of Bill Mallon's children, Barrie, Kevin and Barbara? Pat, now 87 years with an active mind, is keen to make contact with them and possibly meet some of the family as we are planning to take her to New Zealand later this year.

Are you able to provide a contact email or physical address for the Mallons? If privacy is a concern I would be appreciative if you would pass this email on to them to reply directly.

Regards

Michael Knight

I contacted Barrie and Kevin and they were more than happy for me to provide Michael with their contact details. I heard nothing more for nearly a year, wondering if Patricia would manage to meet her family, and then, in March 2016, Michael e-mailed me to inform me that there had indeed been a family re-union. He subsequently sent me this account of the happy occasion:

Vic Jay provided me with contact details of the Alexander Mallon grandchildren and an email exchange of information quickly developed. Patricia was excited about having re-established contact with the Mallon family and quickly accepted our invitation to take her to New Zealand to meet face-to face.

Patricia, with daughters Susan and Beryl (my wife) and I, met up with Barbara Marshall (daughter of Dora May Mallon) in New Plymouth in April 2015. Following a lengthy discussion and exchange of photographs we visited the place of the original Mallon home which is still standing in Bell Block, Taranaki - an emotional experience for Patricia.

Our second meeting was with Barry and Kevin Mallon, including Kevin's family, at his home just south of Christchurch. Barry and Kevin are sons of Bill Mallon. Lots more discussion, photos and looking at some of the service medals of the Mallon family, including Alexander Mallon's Boer War service medal.

Patricia described meeting up with the Mallon with excitement, 'it was well worth the trip, such a wonderful experience'. She said 'it just felt right – was meant to be'. 'No sense of strangers meeting - a feeling of being re-united with family that had not been seen recently'.

Patricia said 'Through Vic and his blog we had the pleasure of meeting up with our relations. Thank you Vic'.

We returned to Australia to celebrate ANZAC Day on this side of the Tasman with a warmth and pride in the service and valour of our New Zealand friends.

As part of her visit Patricia had presented each of the families with some of the poppies she had been knitting for ANZAC day. Barbara wore hers during her Choir performance on ANZAC day 2015, while Kevin and Barry wore theirs when attending ANZAC day ceremonies.

I asked Patricia why the trip to New Zealand and meeting up with the Mallon's was so important to her. She replied 'It joined up the Family Circle. Alexander Mallon, my mother and I, along with a number of other family members, were all born in the same house in Comber Street Paddington, NSW.'

Patricia Colley, left, with Barbara, daughter of Bill's twin sister, Dora May

After the reunion, Kevin spoke on behalf of the New Zealand branch of the Mallon family when he wrote:

> *We enjoyed catching up with Michael and his mum-in-law Pat, we learnt a whole lot about the family that was unknown to us. I know they visited the memorial in Bell Block which includes the names of Jack and Tom, Pat found this quite emotional, as we do when we are in the area. By some coincidence, we live in Knights Road which they found amusing!*

I am pleased to say that my blog had succeeded in bringing together not just the families of long-separated crew members but also the members of a long-separated family.

18 LEGACY: 'MORE THAN JUST A NUMBER'

Bob's contribution to the post-war baby boom, 1951. L to R: Vic, Pam and Bob junior

Despite a couple of near misses the Mallon crew survived, helped by the fact that No. 75(NZ) Squadron was a three-flight squadron and practically double-crewed during the later months of the war. This meant they completed just eight operations in their two months operational service and, with supplies severely disrupted and the Luftwaffe starved of fuel, the dangers from flak and fighters were much reduced. The crew's survival meant that there are more than eighty people alive today who would otherwise never have been born.

Had Bob been successful in his first attempt to enlist in September 1942, he would probably have started his operational duty in the spring of 1944, the worst year for Bomber Command casualties. The two months of the war with the highest number of aircraft lost were June and July 1944, so he would have been expected to complete a tour of thirty or more operations during the most dangerous phase of the air war, with his chance of survival estimated at worse than one in three. There would also have been plenty of time for a second tour had he survived the first. We should be grateful to whoever it was that decided not to recommend him for air crew duties first time round.

The situation was similar for Bill, kicking his heels in the army for nearly a year before embarking on pilot training and then having to wait nearly three more years before being posted to Mepal to commence operational flying. His brothers, on the other hand, moved much more swiftly to the frontline and paid with their lives. Bill's family too, despite their enormous loss, were grateful for the delays that spared Bill.

What I expected to be a brief project to find out a little more about my dad's war service, evolved over four years into so much more than that. I knew that all of the crew had survived but I was shocked to learn the extent to which their lives had been touched by tragedy. As well as Jack and Tom Mallon and Gibson Philp there was Alban Chipling, Hazel Waugh and the old boys of New Plymouth Boys' High School, not to mention all the other members of the squadron who were killed and 'Mac' Baigent, Frank and Stuart Symes and my dad, who all died prematurely in the years following the war.

It is almost impossible, even for close relatives, to grasp the full extent of what is lost when a young person dies. Even if the bereaved are able to articulate their feelings of loss, they will struggle to grasp the magnitude of what might have been. They won't see the children their loved ones might have brought into the world, nor will they witness the fulfilment of any ambitions they may have harboured. Only by looking at a group of survivors such as the Mallon crew, and pondering life without them, is it possible to gain an insight into the scale of their sacrifice.

Although his daughters Ruth and Maryann would probably have gone on to have their families even if Jim had failed to return, their lives would have been missing so much and, of course, Penny would not have been born. Jim was able to take enormous pride in the achievements of his three daughters, seven grandchildren and twelve great grandchildren throughout his life and, despite failing health during his last few years, he still followed their activities with enthusiasm until his death in 2001 at the age of ninety.

Jim's love of sport had certainly rubbed off on his family, with Penny and grandson Jamie going on to represent New Zealand in the Olympic Games. Penny reached the second round and ran a personal best of 52.66 seconds in the 400 metres at Munich in 1972 and Jamie competed in the Men's 470 sailing event at the Athens Olympics in 2004. Both were sports in which Jim had taken a keen interest. He was always very supportive of any family member who made extra effort in any sport and became known at athletics meets throughout the country as he yelled '*Come on kid!*'

Not only did Jim pass on a passion for sport to his family, it seems an interest in aviation was also transmitted. Ruth's son Andy took it as far as flying solo, before the cost of lessons proved too much, but his son Izaak, one of Jim's great grandsons, took it further. He joined Nelson Aviation College in February 2015 at the age of eighteen and, having gained his pilot's licence, he should have his commercial licence by the time this book is published. One can only imagine how proud Jim would have been.

Izaak Ryan taking his dad, Andy, for a short flight, March 2016

Bill Mallon married Lorna several years after returning to New Zealand and they were fortunate enough to spend sixty years together. Their two sons, Barrie and Kevin, whom Kevin describes as 'late starters', have five children between them, all of whom had the opportunity to get to know their grandfather before he died in June 2010, also at the age of ninety. Kevin's daughters, Laura, Emily and Jemma, ranged in age from fourteen to nineteen when Bill died and Barrie's daughter, Catherine, was seventeen. Thomas William, Barrie's son, who was named after both his great uncle and his grandfather, was fourteen.

The loss of their uncles Tom and Jack, whom none of them knew, is still felt deeply within the family, as illustrated by this e-mail, sent by Barrie in 2014, to Paul Warnault, the son of the Mayor of Guînes:

Dear Paul,

Please forgive me as I had intended to write when Vic sent me this email and when I saw it again today it reminded me that I should.

I remember clearly when my father received the letter from your father and he was quite emotional about it and obviously I have kept it along with all the other belongings of his.

I would like to say how grateful our family is that our uncle is being so well cared for still to this day, we are aware of how special he is to your village.

I was interested to read your comment about your father explaining the importance and significance of the buried servicemen in your village.

My brother Kevin has visited the grave a number of years ago and next time I am in England I hope to be able to have the time to visit also.

Both of my father's brothers have meant so much to our families and we will never forget them even though they were both killed long before we were born.

I carry John (Jack) as my middle name, my brother carries Thomas (Tom) as his middle name and my son Thomas carries my father's name William (Bill) as his middle name.

My kind regards to you and your family.

Barrie.

Sadly, Frank Symes was unable to watch his grandchildren grow up as he, like my dad, died at the age of fifty five, but his seven children, Stuart, Yvonne, Graeme, John, Anthony, Stephen and Cecil, are responsible for an enormous legacy of twenty six grandchildren. I doubt there is a grandmother prouder than Winnie in the whole of New Zealand. One of

Frank and Winnie with, L to R, Stuart, Yvonne, Graeme, Antony and John. Stephen and Cecil had not yet been born

their grandchildren, Yvonne's son Warren, who has been my link with the family for the last two years, was just four when his grandad died and, although he can't remember him, he is told that he used to spoil him.

Denis and Winifred Eynstone had one child, Wendy, who was born long after the war in 1958, and she has two sons, Thomas and James. The family lived a considerable distance from their grandparents, who had moved to North Devon after Denis retired, but they always managed a visit at Christmas and during the summer holidays.

Denis and Winifred had several acres of land with sheep, tractors and a sheepdog and lived close to the seaside, so the boys were in their element. Tom, the older brother, would often stay on for a few weeks enjoying the opportunity to do things which he would never have been allowed to do at home, especially with a younger brother in tow. Wendy says that Tom remembers those times with great fondness.

Bob's optimism after the war was dealt a series of body blows. First of all, he felt he had no alternative but to leave a job he loved as a matter of principle over the treatment of some of his comrades in the fire service. He then spent the rest of his life working in some of the most appalling conditions in the chemical industry. The gradual deterioration in the health of his sister Phyllis also took its toll and Bob's support for the Labour Party was facing serious challenges.

Whilst the new Labour government, elected on a tide of post war euphoria, had introduced many of the reforms that Bob and the country were craving, after six years of war the Treasury was almost bankrupt. The U.S. had suddenly and without warning stopped the 'Lend Lease' funding scheme and rationing continued, wages stagnated and people felt their lives were not improving quickly enough. The 1951 general election returned the Conservatives to power, despite the Labour Party still gaining more votes than them and polling their highest percentage of votes ever (48.8%).

The Conservative Party remained in power for the next thirteen years, during which Bob's hopes for lasting peace were shattered, first of all by the continuation of the Korean War, which had started in 1950, and then by the British establishment's brutal attempts to hang on to the last remnants of its empire in Kenya, Malaya and Cyprus.

On my sister's second birthday, the 3rd October 1952, Britain joined the United States and the Soviet Union in the 'nuclear club' when it exploded an atomic bomb close to the Monte Bello Islands off the coast of Australia. To the Labour Party's shame, it was at a secret cabinet committee meeting six years earlier in October 1946, just over a year after bombs were dropped on Hiroshima and Nagasaki, where the wheels had been set in motion. *'We've got to have this thing over here whatever it costs … We've got to have the bloody Union Jack flying on top of it'* was Foreign Secretary Ernest Bevin's comment.

The pattern of post-war life had been set, and I remember as clearly as if it were yesterday my dad saying quietly to my mum after an evening news bulletin in 1956 *'there's going to be another war, you know.'* At nine, I was old enough to understand what war meant, even if I wasn't sure where Suez was, and I had some understanding of the destructive power of nuclear weapons. I hid in the pantry for what must have been an hour, frozen with fear.

Six years later, and with a little more bravado, I experienced similar feelings as I sat with my mates on the school playing field watching the vapour trails of jets overhead and wondering if I would have time to get home if a nuclear attack were launched. It was October 1962 and the height of the Cuban missile crisis.

It is not an exaggeration to say that my young life was marred by the constant fear of war, a legacy of the Cold War which I am sure my dad had not anticipated in those early days of peace in 1945. It meant that he was determined that neither of his sons would be called upon to lay down their lives in the battlefield and his antagonism to any form of militarism was extreme. He wouldn't even agree to our joining the cubs or the scouts.

I grew up to share his abhorrence of war and, over the Easter weekend of 1963, at the age of fifteen, I took part in an anti-nuclear march from Aldermaston to London, a distance of fifty two miles. I am also proud to have taken part in a number of massive demonstrations on the streets of London in opposition to the U.S. war in Vietnam.

Despite what he saw as betrayal by successive Labour governments, and I can only imagine what he would have made of the decision to join the U.S. in the invasion of Iraq in 2003, Bob clung on to his ideals and his passionate belief in peace, internationalism and equality of opportunity. He worked tirelessly through his trade union, the A.E.U. and later the A.U.E.W., to improve working conditions and was a committed anti-racist. As children we knew all about apartheid and the A.N.C long before the Rivonia trials and Nelson Mandela's subsequent imprisonment in 1964.

It is probably true that you can judge a person's character by the people he or she admires, and there were people for whom I remember Bob had enormous respect and admiration. As well as Mandela, these included Paul Robeson, Martin Luther King and even Jimmy Reid, one of the leaders of the Upper Clyde Shipbuilders, all men who had made a stand for what they believed. Muhammad Ali was added to this list, partly because of the grace with which he dismantled his opponents, but also because of the position he took over civil rights and the Vietnam War.

Despite his brief and painful flirtation with the 'noble art', Bob continued to take an interest in boxing and I became enchanted by the names of the fighters he described: Sugar Ray Robinson, Jake LaMotta and the British fighter, Randolph Turpin. I was always Sugar Ray in the 'fights' with my brother after we were given boxing gloves one Christmas.

After the war, my dad was more aware than ever of the power of education to broaden the mind, create opportunities and escape drudgery. The training he had received in the R.A.F. had re-ignited an interest in his own education, and he was soon giving me lessons in basic aerodynamics and the physics of space exploration and avidly following the 'Space Race'. His job was not the one he would have chosen, but he always took pride in his work and I followed his example whenever called upon to carry out jobs that required manual labour – and I became rather skilful at repairing motor vehicles.

It was the unsociable hours of continental shifts and the unhealthy environment in the chemical industry that I believe ultimately killed him. It was only later, after his death, that I fully appreciated the sacrifices he and my mum had made to enable them to support all three of us through higher education, so that we would not have to follow in his footsteps.

My dad never achieved the fulfilment he must have craved but my lifelong love of learning, as well a set of principles by which I try to live my life, is what I consider to be his legacy. As a child, I was immensely proud of the part he played in the war, but it is this legacy that gives me the greatest pride. I suspect this feeling, in one way or another, is shared by the families of all of the Mallon crew.

As I get older and watch my family growing around me, I am thankful that Bob survived the war but incredibly sad that his premature death deprived him of the joy he could have experienced as a grandfather. When he died at the age of fifty five after a long illness, his first grandchild was just twenty months old and his enjoyment of her company must have been severely hampered by his ill health.

My mum lived alone for another thirty seven years, but her life was enriched by her relationship with her six grandchildren who all now live in different parts of the country - Manchester, London, Cheshire, Nottingham, North Yorkshire and even one in Cambridgeshire, just twenty miles from Mepal. None of them is a teacher, the chosen occupation of all

Bob's ten great grandchildren in 2016

three of Bob and Vera's children, but all have gone on to have careers and families of their own. There are now ten great grandchildren to remind us of what a void there would have been had he not survived the war.

In total, the six members of the Mallon crew I know about fathered fifteen children after their military service ended, who in turn have been responsible so far for nearly fifty grandchildren and more than twenty great grandchildren - over eighty people who might never have been born. But the crew's legacy is not just a number. The achievements, values and potential of their descendants are the legacy of the Mallon crew, whilst at the same time serving as a stark and poignant reminder of what might have been for those who were not so lucky.

APPENDIX: NO LET-UP

No.75(NZ) Squadron ground crew refuelling and 'bombing up' a Lancaster at R.A.F. Mepal (picture CH14680 courtesy of I.W.M.)

No. 75(NZ) Squadron was engaged constantly against Germany from 1940 to 1945, flying more sorties than any other Allied bomber squadron and dropping the second largest weight of bombs. It also suffered the second most casualties, with one hundred and ninety three aircraft lost and over eleven hundred aircrew killed.

During March and April 1945, when the Mallon crew was operational, there was no let-up and, despite the reduced effectiveness of German defences, a total of over five hundred aircraft from Bomber Command were lost. March 1945 was the fourth worst month of the war in terms of bombers lost, so it would be wrong to assume that the crew's operations were without risk.

No. 75(NZ) Squadron itself had four of its aircraft shot down during March and April, and it lost three flight engineers, two killed and one captured. Here are the details, with text from the squadron's O.R.B. in italics, of those final operations.

6th March - the squadron provided sixteen Lancasters out of a force of one hundred and nineteen from No. 3 Group Bomber Command for an attack on the **Wintershall oil refinery** in **Salzbergen,** the oldest oil refinery in the world. *'Slight H/F'* (i.e. heavy flak - from large calibre guns) *'was the only opposition'* but one aircraft was lost.

6th/7th March – eighty seven Lancasters from No. 3 Group, including eight from the squadron, and fifty one Mosquitoes from No. 8 Group attacked **Wesel** in two waves, one in the early hours and the other during daylight. *'Flak opposition was slight, no fighters were seen'* and there were no losses. Between the 16th and 19th February **Wesel** had been almost entirely destroyed by the use of impact and air-burst weapons, mainly by No. 3 Group. Three days later the Germans destroyed the 1,950 metre long railway bridge, the last bridge across the Rhine remaining in German hands. The Allies took the town two weeks later but an estimated 97% of its structures had been destroyed by bombing and shelling.

7th/8th March - a single Lancaster took part in mine laying, or 'Gardening', in **Kiel Bay.**

7th/8th March – thirteen of the squadron's aircraft were part of a force of five hundred and twenty six Lancasters and five Mosquitoes, from Nos. 1, 3, 6 and 8 Groups, that bombed targets in **Dessau** in eastern Germany. **Dessau** was home of the **Junkers Aircraft and Engine Works (J.F.M.)** and the first two Ju88-G7 high performance night fighters, the so-called 'Mosquito destroyers', were themselves destroyed before becoming operational. The city was virtually destroyed and over one thousand civilians lost their lives. This was **Bill Mallon**'s first operation, flying '2nd dickey' with **F/L Sid 'Buzz' Spilman**'s crew. *'Flak practically nil in target area, some fighters were seen'* and *'F/L Spilman had a short, inconclusive encounter.'* They were extremely lucky as eighteen Lancasters were lost from other squadrons involved in the operation.

9th March – the Mallon crew's first operation, in which twenty one aircraft from the squadron took part alongside one hundred and thirty eight Lancasters from other squadrons in No. 3 Group, in a raid on the **Emscher Lippe benzol plant** near **Datteln**. '*No opposition was encountered*' although one aircraft was lost.

10th March – one hundred and fifty five Lancasters, twenty one from the squadron including the Mallon crew's, carried out a raid on **Gelsenkirchen**, about 20 km south west of **Datteln** in the Ruhr Valley. The target was the oil refinery at Scholven-Buer. '*There was slight H/F*' and there were no losses.

11th March – twenty one of the squadron's aircraft took part in a 'thousand bomber' raid on **Essen,** involving seven hundred and fifty Lancasters, two hundred and ninety three Halifaxes and thirty six Mosquitoes, a total of one thousand and seventy nine aircraft, making it the largest number so far on a single target. '*Very slight H/F was the only opposition*' and three Lancasters were lost, one of which is pictured here.

12th March - another record number of aircraft on a single raid, this time on **Dortmund,** and this record would not be broken. Seven hundred and forty eight Lancasters, two hundred

One of three Lancasters lost in the 11th March operation explodes over Essen (picture courtesy of the Australian War Museum)

and ninety two Halifaxes and sixty eight Mosquitoes, a total of one thousand one hundred and eight aircraft, dropped nearly five thousand tons of bombs mainly on the centre and south of the city. '*Flak was slight to moderate*' and three Lancasters were lost, none of the twenty one from the squadron.

14th March – one hundred and sixty nine Lancasters bombed oil plants in **Hattingen** and **Datteln**. The twenty from No.

75(NZ) Squadron were among those that targeted the **Heinrich Hutte plants** in **Hattingen** and the squadron lost one of its aircraft. *'Very accurate moderate H/F was met in the run-in and over the target'* and **AA-E** (**PB471**), piloted by **F/L Eric Parsons**, *'was seen to be hit in port inner engine at 16.35 on run in to target and dropped track with port outer also feathered. Port wing caught fire and broke off when just above cloud and was seen spiralling into cloud'*.

All seven of the crew were killed. Five of them were laid to rest in the Reichswald Forest War Cemetery in Kleve, close to the Dutch border in Germany, and two have no known graves and are commemorated at the Runnymede Memorial in Surrey. They are:

- **F/L Eric Parsons** (RAF 185301), pilot (aged 23), Reichswald
- **F/S William Phinn** (RAFVR 1684789), navigator (aged 22), Reichswald
- **F/S Francis Ebbage** (RAFVR 1615600), bomb aimer (aged 21), Runnymede
- **F/S Eric Ramsay** (RAFVR 2205987), wireless operator (aged 20), Reichswald
- **Sgt Charles Longstaff** (RAFVR 1595982), flight engineer (aged 31), Runnymede
- **Sgt John Beard** (RAFVR 3006185), mid-upper gunner (aged 19), Reichswald
- **F/S John Nichol** (RAFVR 1670779), rear gunner (aged 28), Reichswald

17th March – one hundred and sixty seven Lancasters carried out a raid on the benzol plants at both **Dortmund** and **Hüls**. The target of the squadron's twenty aircraft was the Auguste Viktoria benzol plant at **Marl-Hüls**. There was *'slight H/F'* and no losses.

18th March – one hundred Lancasters carried out attacks on **Hattingen** and **Bochum** in the **Ruhr**. The seventeen aircraft from the squadron targeted the coking and benzol plants at Bruchstrasse in **Langendreer**, the most populous district of **Bochum**. Again, *'slight H/F was encountered'* and no aircraft were lost.

20th March – ninety nine Lancasters bombed the railway yards at **Hamm**. *'Some H/F was encountered'* but no aircraft were lost.

21st March - the raid on the railway yards and nearby viaduct at **Münster** was chaotic and tragic, with twelve aircrew losing their lives. There was *'considerable flak'* and three of the squadron's aircraft were brought down, with some desperately trying to avoid bombs from their own aircraft above. The full details of what happened and what errors may have been made will never be known but the circumstances have been explored by several researchers, including Simon Sommerville in his blog.

The three aircraft lost were:

JN-P (RA564) *'failed to return, believed shot down by flak in target area'.* It has been suggested that RA564 was bombing the target when it was struck by a bomb falling from another aircraft flying above. There were no survivors. The body of Warrant Officer Amos was found and buried by advancing U.S. forces and he now lies in the Venray War Cemetery in the Netherlands. The other crew members have no known graves and are commemorated at the Air Forces Memorial at Runnymede in Surrey.

- **F/O Derek Barr** (RAFVR 190947), pilot (aged 29), Runnymede
- **F/S Arthur Oakey** (RNZAF 4213810), navigator (aged 33), Runnymede
- **Sgt Dryden Stewart** (RAFVR 1673061), bomb aimer (aged 22), Runnymede
- **P/O Robert West** (RAFVR 195545), wireless operator (aged 22), Runnymede.
- **F/S Clifford Stocker** (RAFVR 1587275), flight

engineer (aged 30), Runnymede

- **Sgt Bruce Nicholl** (RAFVR 746205), mid-upper gunner (aged 26), Runnymede
- **W/O Alwyn Amos** (RAFVR 1578224), rear gunner (aged 24), Venray War cemetery.

AA-R (LM733) '*failed to return and was seen to break in two over target, possibly due to bombing from above but may have been flak.*' LM733 was bombing the target when it was seen to break into two sections and enter a downward spiral before crashing in flames among trees near Coesfeld at 13.30hrs. The cause of the catastrophic damage was thought to be a combination of flak damage and being struck by a bomb from another aircraft flying above. Two of the crew, the pilot and the bomb aimer, were killed, the others all survived and were captured.

- **P/O Alfred Brown** (RNZAF 429139), pilot (aged 25), Reichswald Forest War Cemetery
- **F/S Arthur Baker** (RNZAF 4214043), navigator, bailed out and survived. P.o.W. camp not known
- **F/S James Wood** (RNZAF 425811), bomb aimer (aged 29), Reichswald Forest War Cemetery
- **F/S Arthur Robson** (RNZAF 4210853), wireless operator, bailed out and survived. Held at Stalag XI-B near Fallingbostel in N.W. Germany
- **F/S R. H. Lawrence** (RAFVR 1607264), flight engineer, bailed out and survived. P.o.W. camp not known
- **Sgt J Grierson** (RAFVR 1593931), mid-upper gunner, bailed out and survived. P.o.W. camp not known
- **Sgt H. Barraclough** (RAFVR 1590144), rear gunner, bailed out and survived. P.o.W. camp not known

AA-T (NG449) '*failed to return, seen to be shot down by flak over the target*'. NG449 came under heavy anti-aircraft fire over the target area and received hits in two engines. It then began breaking up and four of the crew were virtually thrown from the disintegrating aircraft and parachuted to safety. The pilot, bomb aimer and mid-upper gunner all died. It was the Plummer crew's 30th operation and if they had returned safely it would have been the end of their war.

- **F/L Jack Plummer** (RNZAF 42451), pilot (aged 29), killed and buried at Reichswald Forest War Cemetery
- **P/O Arthur 'Tiny' Humphreys D.F.M.** (RNZAF 428244), navigator, bailed out and survived. Probably held at Stalags VI-F and XI-B. It has been reported that he implored the Germans to arrange medical treatment for his badly injured comrades.
- **F/O Edgar Holloway** (RNZAF 429923), bomb aimer (aged 29), killed and buried at Reichswald Forest War Cemetery
- **F/O Joseph Wakerley** (RAFVR 169159), wireless operator, bailed out and survived. Possibly held at Oflag 79 near Braunschweig, Germany
- **Sgt Maurice Fell** (RAFVR), flight engineer, bailed out and survived but was badly injured. Possibly held at Stalag XIB and upon repatriation was treated at the R.A.F. General Hospital at Wroughton in Wiltshire
- **F/O Russell Scott** (RNZAF 428984), mid-upper gunner (aged 23), killed and buried at Reichswald Forest War Cemetery
- **F/S Alexander MacDonald** (RNZAF 426070), rear gunner, bailed out and survived. There are discrepancies in the records of what happened to F/S MacDonald. One story has it that he successfully evaded capture and returned to the U.K. before the end of the war, but the more likely story is that he was also badly injured and captured.

23rd March - Wesel was targeted yet again, this time by eighty Lancasters, eight from the squadron, and three thousand Allied guns on the ground in preparation for

'Operation Plunder', the crossing of the Rhine by the British 2nd Army and the U.S. Ninth Army between the 24th and 27th March. *'Very slight H/F was experienced'* and there were no losses.

25th/26th March - one solitary Lancaster carried out a 'Nickel raid' on **Scheveningen** in **The Hague**, in which thousands of propaganda leaflets were dropped. The operation was *'uneventful'.*

27th March – the Mallon crew's third operation nearly ended in disaster when, on the run in to the target, the port inner engine was hit by flak and they had to complete the operation with three engines. Their target was two benzol plants at Hamm in the north eastern Ruhr and one hundred and fifty Lancasters took part, twenty one from No. 75(NZ) Squadron. *'Very slight H/F was the only opposition encountered'* and there were no losses.

29th March – the crew's fourth operation, involving one hundred and thirty Lancasters, again twenty one from the squadron, was on the **Hermann Goering benzol plant** at **Salzgitter** in Lower Saxony. *'Flak was moderate'* and there were no losses.

4th/5th April - **Merseburg**, about 20 km west of **Leipzig,** was the squadron's next target when three hundred and twenty seven Lancasters and fourteen Mosquitoes hit the **Leuna synthetic oil plant**. Flak was *'moderate to light'* and two Lancasters were lost. This was Bob's fifth operation, this time with F/L Ian Taylor's crew, and one of the twenty one aircraft from 75 (NZ) Squadron lost its Flight Engineer when **Sergeant Doug Williamson** 'fell out' of the aircraft but, as described elsewhere, that story had a happy ending.

9th/10th April – Bob's sixth and the Mallon crew's fifth was another huge operation, this time involving five hundred and ninety one Lancasters from Nos. 1, 3 and 8 Groups bombing targets in Kiel Harbour. *'Flak was moderate', 'there was no fighter opposition'* yet three aircraft were lost, none of the nineteen from the squadron.

On the same night another seven Lancasters from the squadron were sent on a mine laying operation to Kiel.

13th/14th April - another mine laying operation to **Kiel**, this time involving just five of the squadron's aircraft – '*An uneventful trip*'. On the same night, the squadron was part of a force of three hundred and seventy seven Lancasters and one hundred and five Halifaxes that attacked **Kiel** again. '*Flak was slight*' but two Lancasters were lost.

14th/15th April – five hundred Lancasters, including the Mallon crew and twenty four others from No. 75(NZ) Squadron, and twelve Mosquitoes attacked Potsdam, just outside Berlin. '*Flak was slight and bursting well below the stream*'. One Lancaster from another squadron was lost, shot down by a night fighter, and '*AA-T (F/L Baynes) was attacked by two enemy aircraft, believed JU88s, 20 miles S.W. of Potsdam on the homeward journey. The Flight Engineer (Sergeant A. Sliman) was killed by canon shell*'.

The 'Combat report' describes the incident starting at 23.18 whilst flying at about 9,000 feet. The mid-upper gunner Sgt 'Bill' Barnbrook sighted two Ju-88s approaching and gave the order to corkscrew starboard. The first opened fire, damaging the nose of the aircraft and killing Allan Sliman, whilst the other remained some distance away. The attacking aircraft broke away and was given a long burst by the rear gunner, Sgt G. Bentham. No hits were observed. At 23.26 the aircraft was attacked again by two Ju-88s, this time from dead astern, and the rear gunner ordered the pilot to corkscrew starboard once again. He was unable to return fire this time as his hydraulics had been shot away and the rear turret was slightly damaged. In both attacks the second aircraft took no part in the attack, other than acting as a decoy.

Allan Sliman, born in Renfrewshire in Scotland, was thirty nine and had been a professional footballer with Bristol City, Chesterfield and Chelmsford City. At Chesterfield he played two hundred and forty one games over seven seasons, mainly at centre-half. He is considered one of the club's all-time greats and was the foundation on which a side was built to win the Northern Section in the 1935-36 season and establish a place as a Second Division team.

He joined Chelmsford City in 1938 and was appointed captain. He also served as player manager for five months and played a vital part in their F.A. Cup run that

season. The picture above, from the Chelmsford War Memorial website, shows Allan, on the right, shaking hands with the Darlington captain before kick-off in the second round – Chelmsford won 3-1. They were eventually knocked out by Birmingham City, losing 6-0 in the fourth round.

He enlisted in 1943 and commenced his flight engineer training a few weeks after Bob in 1944. Having only arrived at Mepal on the 1st April, Allan was killed on his and his crew's first operation. He left behind a widow, Gladys Rosina Sliman.

18th April – nine hundred and sixty nine aircraft, including six hundred and seventeen Lancasters, three hundred and thirty two Halifaxes and twenty Mosquitoes, carried out a devastating attack on the tiny island of **Heligoland**. Several theories have been put forward to explain why such a massive blow was needed against such a small and relatively unimportant target, but there were submarine pens, anti-aircraft batteries and a small airstrip on the island. Three Halifaxes were lost. The following day, another thirty six aircraft from Nos. 9 and 617 Squadrons attacked coastal batteries on the island with 12,000 lb 'Tallboy' bombs.

20th April – the Mallon crew's penultimate operation involved one hundred Lancasters bombing the fuel storage depot, the docks and the railway system at **Regensburg**. Flak was *'slight but accurate'* and one aircraft was lost.

22nd April - the squadron's penultimate operation, just over two weeks before V.E. Day, was part of a huge daylight raid on the south eastern suburbs of the city of **Bremen,** in North West Germany, in preparation for the advance of the British XXX Corps. Six hundred and fifty two Lancasters, one hundred Halifaxes and sixteen Mosquitoes took part, but the raid was hampered by cloud and by smoke and dust from bombing, and the Master Bomber called off the raid before Nos. 1 and 4 Group could attack. The city was taken just four days later, on the 26th April.

'Flak from Wilhelmshaven and Bremen was at intervals moderate and very accurate but no fighters were seen'. Two Lancasters were lost and **Squadron Leader J. Parker's** aircraft **AA-P (NF935),** one of twenty one from the squadron, was struck by flak at 17,500 feet over Wilhelmshaven as it was returning from Bremen. The aircraft returned safely, but flight engineer **Sergeant Roy Stanley Clark** of the R.A.F.V.R. was killed. He was twenty two and is buried in Chingford Mount cemetery in the London borough of Waltham Forest. He left behind a widow, May Ethel Eileen Clark, in Clapton, London.

24th April – the crew's and the Squadron's final operation saw twenty one Lancasters from the squadron detailed to attack railway targets at **Bad Oldesloe** in northern Germany. *'No opposition was encountered but slight flak was seen over the Dutch coast'.*

From the **29th April** to the **8th May**, the squadron was involved in 'Operation Manna', dropping supplies on The Netherlands in the areas around Delft, Rotterdam and The Hague. Then, from the **9th May** to the **23rd May,** it helped repatriate approximately two thousand prisoners of war. Aircraft would fly to **Juvincourt**, in north eastern France, and each one would carry twenty four released prisoners, many of them Australians and New Zealanders.

During May 1945 dozens of Belgian refugees were also repatriated, including a two months old baby, and throughout May and June so-called 'post-mortem' operations were carried out to *'check German radar equipment'*. From the **23rd May** to the **19th July** crews were tasked with taking official photographers, ground crew and 'top brass' to *'view the effects of the bombing offensive'*. These trips were widely known as 'Baedeker' operations, named in memory of the 1942 German bombing raids on British tourist destinations featured in the Baedeker Travel Guides. Jim, who referred to these flights as 'Cook's Tours', described one of them in a letter to his wife, featured in Chapter 9.

POSTSCRIPT

At the culmination of this project, I am left with one regret. Despite writing dozens of letters, searching the internet for hours and even spending money on a leading people tracing company, I have been unable to locate the family of the crew's mid-upper gunner. Don Cook, born in 1924 or 1925, possibly in the London area, remains a constant reminder that the internet does **not** have all the answers. This project will not be complete until I have found him.

ABOUT THE AUTHOR

Vic Jay was born in 1947, two years after the end of the war. He studied at the University of Liverpool in the 1960s before training in Nottingham to be a teacher. He went on to teach in his home town of Grimsby for thirty eight years before retiring and embarking on a number of projects, including this one.

Made in the USA
San Bernardino, CA
11 November 2017